Praise for *Faith of Cranes*

"*Faith of Cranes* is a love song to the beauty and worth of the lives we are able to lead in the world just as it is, troubled though it be. Lentfer's storytelling achieves its joys and universality not via grand summations but via grounded self-giving, familial intimacy, funny friendships, attentive griefs, and full-bodied immersion in the Alaskan rainforest. The writing is honest, intensely lived, and overflowing with heart: broken, mended, and whole."

—David James Duncan,
author of *The Brothers K* and *God Laughs & Plays*

"*Faith of Cranes* is an astonishing book—lyrical, honest, filled with life and death and beauty and heartbreak, and set in the gorgeously fertile, rainforested islands of Alaska. Hank Lentfer's story is that of a man who discovers his place in the world—and the peace that long eluded him—in the grip of his young daughter's hand, and under the bugling cries of high-flying cranes. Do not miss this book."

—Scott Weidensaul,
author of *Of a Feather* and *Living on the Wind*

"*Faith of Cranes* is a tear-jerking, heart-breaking, spirit-lifting song. Elegantly and precisely written, it sings of one man's love of place, home, and family. Lentfer's writing shines light on the often dim landscape of the ongoing desecration of the environment at the hands of humanity."

—Lynn Schooler,
author of *The Blue Bear* and *Walking Home*

"*Faith of Cranes* is a truly beautiful book, as purely Alaskan as nagoonberries and venison jerky. Exquisitely written—authentic, wise, funny, quirky, honest, heartbreaking—it reveals a man whose soul is as wild as the far north country where his life is anchored."

—Richard Nelson,
author of *The Island Within*

"Hank Lentfer's *Faith of Cranes* is the best kind of memoir—one that illuminates a particular life in a particular place but extends well beyond the personal to explore big issues about family, community, and how we can live with gratitude and hope. Lentfer, a major new voice not just in Alaska writing but in literary nonfiction and philosophy of place, is the storyteller you would want at your campfire. You will never see a migrating crane—or any other bird—in quite the same way again."

—Nancy Lord,
former Alaska Writer Laureate, author of *Beluga Days* and *Early Warming*

"How do we summon the faith, maybe the courage, to move toward a future in a world so grievously threatened? *Faith of Cranes* is Hank Lentfer's answer. Authentic and essential, heart-wrenching yet luminous with hope, Lentfer writes in the tradition of America's best naturalist–philosophers like Sigurd Olsen and Terry Tempest Williams. His story of wild Alaska is one-of-a-kind—courageous, funny, wise, and beautiful."

— Kathleen Dean Moore,
author of *The Pine Island Paradox* and *Wild Comfort*

"Read *Faith of Cranes* for the descriptions of nature, surely, but read it also for the eloquent love story, for the celebration of fatherhood, for the portraits of mentors, and for the meditations on the ethics of eating our fellow beings. In these pages, you can witness one man's discovery of the right place, the right partner, and the right path."

— Scott Russell Sanders,
author of *A Conservationist Manifesto*

FAITH OF CRANES

FAITH OF CRANES

Finding Hope
and Family in Alaska

By HANK LENTFER

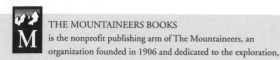
THE MOUNTAINEERS BOOKS
is the nonprofit publishing arm of The Mountaineers, an
organization founded in 1906 and dedicated to the exploration,
preservation, and enjoyment of outdoor and wilderness areas.

1001 SW Klickitat Way, Suite 201, Seattle, WA 98134

First edition, 2011

10 9 8 7 6 5 4 3 2 1

Distributed in the United Kingdom by Cordee, www.cordee.co.uk

Manufactured in the United States of America

Copy Editor: Kim Runciman
Cover, Book Design, and Layout: Karen Schober

Cover photograph (top) courtesy of Sean Neilson © 2011
Cover photograph (bottom) courtesy of Kim Heacox © 2011
Frontispiece courtesy of Kim Heacox © 2011

Library of Congress Cataloging-in-Publication Data
Lentfer, Hank.
 Faith of cranes : finding hope and family in Alaska / Hank Lentfer.
— 1st ed.
   p. cm.
 ISBN 978-1-59485-639-6 (pbk.)—ISBN 978-1-59485-640-2 (ebook)
1. Lentfer, Hank. 2. Lentfer, Hank—Family. 3. Gustavus
(Alaska)—Biography. 4. Fathers—Alaska—Gustavus—Biography. 5.
Conservationists—Alaska—Gustavus—Biography. 6. Sandhill
crane—Alaska—Gustavus Region. 7. Gustavus Region
(Alaska) —Environmental conditions. 8. Fatherhood—Psychological
aspects—Case studies. 9. Hope—Case studies. I. Title.
 F914.G87L46 2011
 979.8'2—dc23

 2011019149

for
Linnea Rain

The opposite of faith is not doubt; it is certainty.
—ANNE LAMOTT

Hawk Larson

TABLE OF CONTENTS

Prologue

CRANES AND COTTONWOODS

CRANES FLEW INTO MY LIFE one evening in late September. I was nailing the last board onto the roof of my house. Cottonwood leaves, yellow and dry, dropped onto the wood while I worked. The flock poured in from the northwest and passed so close that the whistle of wind through feathers mixed with their throaty calls. I teetered on the steep roof, hammer dangling from my hand, staring at the birds. I'd heard cranes before but not from the top of my own home, not from the place I intended to spend the rest of my life.

I was twenty-five when I sank that last nail, gathered my tools, and climbed down the ladder. Every year since, without fail, when the cottonwood leaves color and curl, those ancient birds flood the sky over our home. They drift in waves, tired after a long day's flight, gray wings set against the sunset. Touching down, they flap hard to slow the pull of gravity, their stick-thin legs outstretched to meet the earth. From the porch, if the winds are still, I can hear the birds chattering through the night.

They might stay for a day, a week, waiting for fair winds and rising thermals. When the time is right, a single crane crouches and leaps to the air, followed by another, and another, and then a thousand more. They flap and glide in a growing spiral, calling as if lifted by their own sound. Lying on my back alongside our garden, I stare into a whirlpool of wings. At the thermal's top, the cranes spill out in a long, fluid skein, the current of a collective compass. Not until the birds slip from view, pulling the last voice with them, do I get up, brush the grass from my shirt, and try to remember what I was doing with my day.

Our home sits at the forested edge of a wide meadow about halfway between the cranes' Arctic nests and their California wintering grounds. Having built our little house ourselves, my wife and I view the crude construction with great affection. We carry our water in buckets and get the morning weather report on the way to the outhouse. Anya and I hammered our house together with nails and the naive belief that by staying put we could avoid the urbanization of America—could live, somehow, in peaceful isolation. When I fell in love with cranes, I had no idea they would lead me to the very thing I was trying to escape.

I was born here in Alaska, raised through the fat years of timber and oil, when entire watersheds were cut and shipped to Japan and the long pipeline transformed the last frontier into the next opportunity. A visiting Vermont friend once told me, "You can stay and preside over the destruction of Alaska. I'd rather return home and help with the restoration of the Northeast." He's got a point. No one from Vermont is pounding the podium chanting, "Drill, baby, drill!"

I left Alaska for a few years to study ecology at a small university in Washington. My ornithology professor loved birds as much as any human can love another creature. Frustrated with the university's minivans, Steve spent his own money on a yellow school bus so he could take the whole class to his favorite places. He drove with binoculars pinned to his eyes. At the sight of a horned grebe in a slough or hawk owl on a branch, he'd slam on the brakes, swing open the doors, and we'd all tumble out to gawk. His enthusiasm for the feathered was infectious. So was his despair.

In lecture hall one day, we started talking about the notion of progress. What is linear? Repetitive? Guided by evolution? God? Greed? Steve listened quietly to his students trying to sound scholarly. In a pause in the banter he said, "Progress is the inevitable diminution of beauty over time." Steve was a big man, stiff and gray with age. He made the pronouncement, took off his glasses, rubbed his eyes, passed a lingering gaze over his students, then turned and clomped out the emergency exit. There was an hour of class time left, so we hung out for a bit. When it was obvious he was not coming back, we gathered up our books and left.

Inevitable diminution of beauty over time. Four years of college and this is the one line I can quote verbatim. Steve not only delivered the verdict with some dramatic flair but lived beneath its weight. We could hear it in his voice as he talked of the year Interstate 5 was built across the wetlands where he'd hunted as a boy. We could see it in the way he drank too much beer, slurring and stumbling at class potlucks. We could sense it in the way a rhapsody about the marvels of migration would suddenly flip into a rant about the stupidity of politicians. We'd feel it when a lab period dedicated to the architecture of a hummingbird's nest would spiral into curses against the engineers of dikes and dams.

If my professor was right (and I believed he was), if the beauty of the world was to be eclipsed by chainsaws and chain stores, if the gears of the industrial revolution remained hell-bent on processing the gorgeous into the useful, then having a child made no sense. The diminution of beauty over time assumes the world's beauty is finite, assumes a future of darkness. In such a world, the greatest act of parental love is not to become a parent at all.

———

Ten million years ago, a roiling cloud of volcanic ash obliterated the sun. It fell fast, like an avalanche of black snow, suffocating the animals of the Great Plains beneath ten feet of abrasive powder. Today, at an excavation site in Nebraska, teams of graduate students slowly scrape and sweep through the black earth surrounding an ancient watering hole. The world emerging beneath their tools looks more like the African savanna than the farm country of the Midwest. The students have uncovered an entire herd of hippos gathered for a drink. Around the outskirts of the oasis are the remains of rhinos; three-toed horses; deer-like animals with twisting, forward-leaning horns; and long-necked camels larger than present-day giraffes. The fine ash yields the delicate details of bones and even the impressions of feathers. Of all the bizarre critters rising from that ash, only the graceful skeleton of the sandhill crane looks familiar to our modern-day eyes.

Since that blast, cranes have made millions of migrations over a changing continent. Most of the species that survived the volcano were later killed by a prolonged drought that shuffled the composition of North American fauna. The cranes watched the demise of rhinos, camels, and hippos. They watched trans-American forests and woodlands give way to grassland prairie. They saw glaciers stretch from coast to coast, retreat and return, again and again. They witnessed the arrival and extinction of woolly mammoths and short-faced bears, saber-toothed tigers and giant sloths. Crane calls greeted the first humans spreading south down the continent from Beringia. In recent decades, the oldest species of bird on the planet has watched the lights of cities scatter across the country like embers from a great fire.

In all the years living beneath the spectacle of sandhills, I never followed them south. I did not want to see what I knew I'd find in California. Not until a new life began to stir within the ocean of Anya's belly did I buy a ticket. I wanted my child to grow up beneath the rhythm of cranes, wanted her heart to swell, like mine, with the passing of each raucous flock. But I worried about teaching my kid to love something I could not protect. I needed to know, before my child was born, whether she might grow to know a silent sky.

So I went to the Central Valley and saw cranes picking through rows of corn being converted to rows of condos. After surviving asteroids, volcanoes, and continental glaciations, cranes will not likely survive the human transformation of the planet. We deny the data and pump out CO_2 without pause. We cling to the suicidal notion of perpetual progress. In this country alone, over 3.2 million acres a year are lost to urban sprawl. That's three hundred sixty-two acres each hour. Species are going extinct every day. My professor was right: beauty is, indeed, bleeding bit by bit from this world. My daughter may well live to know a silent sky.

But this is more than a story of loss. It is the story of how I came to believe my professor was also wrong; a story of how cranes, deer, and one little black-haired, blue-eyed girl taught me that running from loss is a race you can win only by standing still; a story of how one man, blinded to present beauty by the fear of an ugly future, regained his sight.

Chapter One

BUTTERSCOTCH OATMEAL

WE STOOD SHOULDER TO SHOULDER around the wood stove, rubbing our hands, thawing our bellies, and then turning around to defrost our backs. Frank stuffed more wood into the firebox and another cookie into his mouth. He passed them round—a triple batch of oatmeal with butterscotch bits and plenty of sugar. Frank had baked them the previous night back in Juneau, before the winds picked up. Anya took a half. Richard grabbed one. I scooped two.

"I feel like a rotisserie chicken," Frank said, spinning by the stove. I laughed, choking on my cookie and spitting crumbs across the cabin's rough plank floor. Anya laughed at me. Richard laughed at Anya. It wasn't all that funny. But we were drunk on the feel of blood returning to near-frozen fingers and toes, giddy to be out of the boat, off the water, and into that tiny palace of a cabin. We giggled our way through a round of cocoa and then a round of tea. Even after I thawed, I stayed near the stove, drawn as much to Anya's smile as to the wood's heat.

It was hard to believe I'd met Anya only that morning. The clouds were just easing from the night's dark when my dad had dropped me at Anya's beachside house twenty miles north of Juneau. When I'd rounded the corner of the house a beautiful woman had hopped over a snow-covered rock, tugged off her mitten, and thrust her hand toward me. "You must be Hank. Anya Maier, good to meet you." She was bundled in thick layers of winter clothes topped with a dark green suit of heavy rain gear. Her eyes wrinkled against round cheeks pushed high by a wide grin, bordered by tufts of jet-black hair. I dropped my backpack and fumbled with my own glove. Her grip was quick, firm. Before I could get my glove back on, Anya had slung my pack over her shoulder, grabbed my rifle, and trudged down the beach.

Empty-handed, I had followed her over the seaweed-covered rocks to the skiff. Frank Maier, Anya's father, stood in the eighteen-foot aluminum boat and stowed the gear between the seats as Richard Carstensen, another of Frank's hunting buddies, handed it to him. Since meeting Frank several years before, I'd often made excuses to visit him. He was easy to find since he rarely left the yard alongside the funky old beach house he shared with his wife, Judy Maier. His drafting table was set up in a renovated old shed next to the house. Whenever I showed up, he'd set down his pencil and ruler.

"Cup of tea? Cookies?" Sitting in the worn comfort of his home, he'd ask questions, listen to my ideas, and share his own with an earnestness that made me feel twice my age.

More than being at home, Frank liked to be in the woods. He owned a cabin (built with his father in the 1950s) on Admiralty Island, a forty-five-minute boat ride from Juneau. Taped to Frank's office wall was a list of potential hunter buddies willing to make the trip. I was thrilled when my name was added. I was just eighteen, a high-school senior. Anya was a few years older, home from college on Christmas break. I could not have known it at the time, but meeting your lover's parents first is a slick approach to courtship. *They* introduced us. What could they say when, years later, Anya brought me home for dinner and I stayed until breakfast?

———

With all the gear stowed, we clambered into the skiff and shoved off. Frank yanked the starter cord several times before the frozen outboard popped and sputtered to life. He eased the boat out of the protected waters of Lena Cove into choppy seas marching up Stephens Passage from the south. Slowing the boat, he scanned the white-topped waves. "What do you guys think?" he asked. "If we're going to turn around, this is the place to do it."

"Looks good to me," I said, full of bravado.

"Whatever you think, Daddy," Anya said.

Richard stayed quiet, glancing from me to Frank to the waves.

"If it doesn't get any worse, we'll be all right," Frank said, as much to himself as anyone else. We drove on, the water beating a tight, jarring rhythm against the hull. Ravens played in the wind, twisting and soaring past the homes lining Auke Bay. When we left the houses behind and nosed into the wide reach of Young Bay the water was rougher but not yet dangerous. Halfway across, the gusts quickly tightened into a steady driving whine. Tendrils of wind-driven foam streaked across the dark water. The skiff climbed steeply over each wave and slammed hard into the troughs. Sheets of salt spray doused the boat as the bow punched through each wall of water. Frank alone squinted into the deluge. The rest of us had our backs to the wind, faces drawn into the lee of our own bodies.

"We're committed now!" Frank shouted into the wind. "Don't think we can run with this on our stern." Richard made his silent eye contact. I grinned at Anya. Anya gripped the gunwale with mittened hand and forced a smile back at me. Frank watched the waves with strained concentration.

The rain of sea spray froze in a thickening sheet on our gear, the seats, our shoulders. I watched the lettering on the outboard—*Johnson Workhorse—40 hp*—slowly fade beneath a growing gauze of ice. Nobody spoke. As icy waters tumbled past, we each clung to whatever shred of comfort we could find in the distance of our own thoughts. Our course was, literally, in Frank's hands. The rest of us could do little more than hope and wait and hold on as the skiff bucked and shuddered its way across the bay.

My first clue that we were close was Frank's smile. "I think we're going to make it," he beamed, moments before he cut the engine and the keel ground into the gravel beach. When Richard hopped over the bow, ice cracked from his back like shattered porcelain. I tapped on the back of Anya's head, her hat like a glazed helmet. We stomped and jogged on the beach, breaking free from our icy coats, forcing blood into stiff limbs, celebrating the solidity of rocks under our feet. We hustled gear to the tree line and dragged the boat above the waves before turning toward the shelter of the cabin.

———

The next morning the winter sun was slow to penetrate the thick forest canopy, leaving plenty of time for coffee and cinnamon rolls. I couldn't admit it to the older hunters, or even myself, but I was nervous about the coming day. I'd been hunting for years, had killed a few deer, but always with my dad right there to answer my questions before they were ever asked. Leaving Juneau the day before, I had been proud to be on my own. Now, making a sandwich to take into the woods, I wished I were packing two lunches instead of one.

"Ani, where should we go today?" Frank asked, pulling thick wool pants over his long underwear. "How about that alder slide up at nine hundred feet where we found that big guy last year?"

"I'll follow wherever you go," Anya said, slipping a pair of binoculars over her head. "Lead the way."

"How about you, Richard?" Frank asked.

"I'll take south of the creek as usual. Maybe work the edge of those muskegs."

I took my rifle from the rack and fiddled with the bolt. "Hank, there's nice open woods straight behind the cabin," Frank offered. "Keep climbing until you see good sign. This snow is so crunchy they'll hear you coming a mile away. I'd sit as long as you can stand the cold."

Outside, the subzero air bit my nose with the sharpness of puppy teeth. We stood in a loose circle, breath clouds rising like cigarette smoke.

"See you all around dark," Richard said.

"First one back, stoke that stove and brew the coffee," Frank said. "And don't eat all the cookies."

"Good luck," Anya said, giving Richard a hug. She slapped my back with her heavy leather mitten and beamed a wide smile mirrored in her father's face. I watched the others go, then turned past the cabin with its beckoning smoke trailing from the chimney. Every third or fourth step plunged me thigh-deep through the crusted snow, rattling the still woods with a sound like breaking glass. After the first hill, I felt a drop of sweat slip down my spine. I stopped to settle my breath and unzip my coat, hearing my father's reminder that to stay warm you have to keep cool. In the decades Dad spent traveling with Eskimos across the Arctic ice, he learned that sweat kills; get in a hurry and you'll never be able to stop without freezing to death.

I moved, just shy of sweating, through the gray columns of hemlock trees. At the top of a steep slope, I kicked a chair into the icy snow, leaned my rifle against a tree, and sat. I scanned the wide span of trees below and then dug for my lunch. One sandwich and two cookies later, tendrils of cold reached down my collar and up my legs. I forced myself to sit, willing an animal to move through the frozen forest. When the first shivers rippled along my ribs, I decided to move on. As I stood, my eyes locked on twin lobes directly below me. I could not see the body. Not even the neck. Just the curve of the skull and the loops of ears. She was looking downhill, ears twitching as she chewed her cud.

Pressing the rifle against the tree trunk, I found the deer in the scope's circle. I squeezed the trigger, the deer turned her head, the explosion shattered the cold. She stepped into full view, still looking downhill. I chambered another round, steadied the crosshairs between the ears, and squeezed the trigger. But this time the gun didn't fire. I slammed the bolt, ejected the shell, jammed another bullet forward. Squeeze—click. Another bullet. Another squeeze. Another click. My last bullet. Another click.

Rifle empty, I watched the deer through the scope. She turned her head, tongue hanging through the space where her lower jaw should be. My heart leaped. My lungs gulped for air as though I'd just sprinted a mile. I ripped off a glove to grab a dull gold bullet from the snow, the primer dimpled, defective. I put the bullet between my lips to reach for another and instantly felt my mistake. After tearing the frigid metal from my mouth, I tasted the salty sting of blood. A child's folly. A tongue-on-the-frozen-doorknob dare you never do twice.

I reloaded and clicked through the rounds, once, twice, a third time. Still the gun refused to fire. I dug through my pack for the box of extra shells my father told me to always carry. I dumped my gear on the snow, wishing I was wrong; wishing my box of bullets was not on the cabin table where I had left them.

The deer stood next to a huge hemlock. I eased sideways to put the gray trunk between us. Out of sight, I crept toward the deer, useless rifle in one hand. When I reached the tree, I took a deep breath. Sweat tickled beneath the edge of my wool hat. The deer had not moved. Just fifteen feet away, blood speckled the snow beneath her head like beads of red wax. I stepped from the tree and she turned to look. We stared—me at the drips falling from her dangling tongue, the hideous shape of her once-beautiful face redrawn by missing bone and flesh; she at . . . what? I can't say what the deer saw. She stared back at me, seemingly calm, perhaps shocked beyond panic and pain, unable to make sense of my predatory profile.

When she turned downhill again I followed her gaze to the miniature shape of her fawn. I gripped the rifle barrel like a bat. Four, maybe five, quick steps, a sharp swing, the crush of bone beneath wood, and I could end what I wished had never started. I raised the gun, took two steps, faltered, and watched the deer step away. Her gait was deliberate, slow. I might have caught her if I had run but I stood, frozen in place. She paused now and then, looking back. Her fawn stared at me for a few long minutes before gingerly following its mother.

I watched them both weave away between the trees, the black flags of tail flicking on their white rumps. When they were out of sight, I jammed my rifle in the snow and launched into motion. I slid and tumbled downhill, pulled by gravity and pushed by anger at my own stupidity. I hit the beach a half mile from the cabin. Hat in hand, coat wide open, I jogged over the tide-cleared gravel, hair and clothes matted with sweat. The cabin was cold and empty. The box of bullets was there, on the table next to the plastic tub of cookies.

I put the ammo in a pocket, stuffed a cookie in my mouth, and stomped back into the woods. I'd find my gun, follow the blood trail, kill the deer, salvage some thread of pride. I trudged uphill, trying to outpace my embarrassment. I climbed too high and cut back down, scanning each hillside for my pack and rifle. The dim sun hung low behind a thin gray sky. I pushed through the last hour of light, sidehilling, climbing, sliding, searching for a familiar patch of forest that would tell me I was close.

At dark I gave up. I walked the beach slowly. No rifle, no pack, no deer. Just a story I wished I didn't have to tell. Lantern light glowed in the cabin window. Frank's laughter and Anya's soft voice drifted, muted, through the glass. I stood in the dark woods until my sweat-soaked clothes forced me into the warmth.

While Anya diced and stirred around the stove, creating a pot of soup and plate of biscuits, I described my day. Frank had heard my shot, was surprised to come down and not find a deer hanging alongside the cabin. "I bet the cold thickened the oil on your rifle," Frank offered. "Made the firing pin stick." Richard said he'd go out with me in the morning and find my stuff, search for the deer. No one asked why I had not followed my own tracks back to the rifle. No one said that only a fool could lose his way in a snowy forest.

We ate beneath the hissing glow of the lantern casting stark shadows on the cabin walls. After the dishes were washed and dried, Frank slid the tub of cookies onto the plywood table. I grabbed a few and joined Anya in a nest of sleeping bags piled in a dark corner. My head found her lap. Her fingers found my hair. Under Anya's tender touch, I listened to Frank and Richard pour through memories of previous hunts. They talked of their own missed shots, wounded animals, and stupid moves as if I were not listening; as if I didn't need them to make room for me in that wide stretch of stories.

Chapter Two

ALPINE SUNRISE

DAD ALWAYS CARRIED THE BIGGEST LOAD. He led the way up the mountain, following bear tracks along the salmon stream and deer trails on the forested ridge. When, as a little kid, I complained about my rain-saturated clothes, Dad would remind me that my skin was waterproof, nothing to worry about. Whenever he sensed my young legs growing overly weary, he'd call for a break.

"I'm about ready for a breather. How about you?"

We'd drop our packs and lean against a tree trunk while Dad rummaged for the snacks. It was always the same: a bag of trail mix, one of those huge Hershey bars, a block of cheese, and a tube of summer sausage. We'd eat in tired silence, passing the bag of trail mix between us, slicing thick slabs of cheese and meat with a hunting knife. Sometimes we napped, lying back in the moss, our heads on a pack, ball caps pulled over our eyes. I'd wake to Dad's voice. "Mountain's waiting for us. What do you say we keep climbing?" I'd rub my eyes and pretend not to notice that my pack was now lighter, pretend that my sleeping pad had always been strapped to the outside of Dad's load.

Years later, I learned that while I hustled to keep pace with Dad's long legs, Anya was trailing after her dad on the neighboring ridge. As kids we had no way of knowing those parallel hunts would one day converge. Looking back, it seems inevitable our lives would someday bridge that valley. Odd that it took so long.

As Frank and Anya pitched their tent on their favorite alpine knoll, Dad and I stretched our tarp between gnarled spruces huddled along the edge of a quiet, subalpine bog. We dipped water from a round dark pool alive with water striders and diving beetles. We cooked over a small smoky fire and boiled water for cocoa in a coffee can rigged with a wire handle. We slept side by side, curled in sleeping bags beneath that tiny tarp.

Waking in the dark, we used flashlights to prepare our packs for the climb to the top. As we slipped free of the last trees and entered the twilight expanse of the alpine, we began the silent search for deer. In the early years, when I was too young to carry a gun, I followed Dad's crouched stance and whispered tones as he crept within range. I held a leg or tugged on the hide as Dad transformed the deer into a bundle of meat. At age thirteen, I carried a rifle up the mountain and shot my first deer. With Dad's guidance, I skinned and gutted, reaching my hands deep into the warm chest to pull free the heart and lungs. Always, as we worked, ravens circled above, dropping through twisting somersaults and calling in anticipation of the coming meal. We loaded the meat in packs and left the head, hide, guts, and bones for the black birds and brown bears.

Back at camp we laid the meat out to cool beneath the tarp. We stayed up late, roasting cube after cube of venison on sharpened sticks held over the glowing coals. I recall the greasy grit of salt between my fingers as I seasoned each bite, the fluttering of bats in and out of the campfire's light, stars reflected in the still pond as I dipped water for more cocoa, the chilling expanse of the dark mountain harboring those lumbering bears, the comfort of having Dad all to myself. We slept with the meat between us. "Best way to keep the bears away," Dad said, zipping his bag up to his chin.

Memories from those short trips push aside a thousand routine child-hood days. Something about the effort of the climb, the hard ground at my back, rain blowing past the tarp's edge, the earth's slow spin into daylight. Something about witnessing the deer's death, holding and eating a heart the size of my own, imagining the bonds in my own body while dissecting the deer's, feeling warm flesh turn cold. Something about the intimacy with my father, faith that he would find the way home when we were lost, being held inside his coat against his warm chest when the damp of my own clothes threatened hypothermia, smiling together as dawn set fire to the clouds.

———

After I left home for college and Mom and Dad moved away from Juneau, we missed a few hunts, the logistics just too much. But the mountain's gravity pulled us back. Sometime in my twenties I started leading the way, carrying the bigger pack, calling for a snack break to allow Dad's creaky knees to rest. When I was a kid, Dad seemed invincible. Later, his aging body added a sense of preciousness to our time in the woods. We knew that this one, or the next, might be our last climb.

Coming down from a successful hunt several years ago, the bulk of the deer's weight on my shoulders, I called for a break. Dad agreed, leaning his rifle and walking stick against a tree and slipping out from underneath his load. We sat within arm's reach in the quiet light of the forest, passing scraps of chocolate and crumbs of trail mix back and forth. Pillars of hemlock trunks rose pale and still from the hillside beneath us. The sea, a thousand feet below, sparkled brightly beyond the dark forest. A half-hearted, late-summer whistle of a varied thrush trailed through the quiet woods. Passing Dad the bag, I was startled to see a tear slide across his cheek. He wiped it away with a quick flip of his hand and tossed a few peanuts in his mouth. I doubt he would have said anything had I not asked. When he finally answered, his was voice choked with emotion. "I feel you falling in love with this place," he said, staring off through the forest. We finished the trail mix, chewing our way through the awkward emotions.

Dad's love and lament for wild country was inherited: conflicting emotions born on cold Montana mornings while hunting white-tails with his own father along river bottoms now sliced into subdivisions. My grandfather was born in 1899, a few years before the first strip of hardtop road was laid down in far-away Boston. By the time he finished grade school, the Wright brothers had lumbered a plane into the sky and Henry Ford had rolled out the first of fifteen million Model Ts. His own children were in school when early televised images reported tens of thousands of Japanese killed by a bomb called "Fat Boy."

Through the decades of progress, Grandpa Hank and Grandma Rose came and went from their little home on Second Street in Livingston, Montana. They raised two children, went to church, and tended a garden. On weekends Grandpa shared his favorite fishing holes, duck ponds, and deer pastures with his growing son. While father and son hunted and fished through the seasons, that ten-mile strip of Boston-born asphalt crept across the continent, morphing into interstates, parking lots, and runways.

As a kid, I didn't see much of my grandparents. The trip between Alaska and Montana was too long and too expensive to make more than once every few years. Rarity sharpens memory; snippets from each visit stand clear. The earliest is pinned to the acrid smell of tanned hides and animal fur permeating the jumbled workspace of Grandpa's taxidermy shop. "Come look at this, Hankie," said Grandpa, sliding open a series of narrow drawers. I peered in at the marble eyes: the oblong pupils of bobcats, the big globes of deer, the beady circles of bears. Later, Grandad led me down the steep stairs to the cellar. "Listen to this." With a stick he tapped a metal garbage can, which instantly tingled with an electrifying buzz. He tilted the lid so I could peek at the entwined bodies of rattlesnakes writhing in the depth of the can.

Grandpa was an artist, a craftsman. He shaped papier-mâché into the skulls of mule deer and black bears. He smoothed the feathers of teal and widgeons into preened perfection. He painted the taut skin of rainbow trout with lifelike vibrancy. He made necklaces from the vertebrae of snakes and claws of owls. I was fascinated by it all, too young to see the irony in his affection for life finding expression in replicas of the living.

Grandpa's curiosity about critters ran as strong through my dad as the currents of all those Montana trout streams. As a kid, he read and reread Jack London's Alaska stories. He listened to the bravado of hunters in the taxidermy shop recounting the endless herds of caribou and roaming packs of wolves. After high school, Dad signed up for biology classes at Montana State College in Bozeman. He stayed on for a master's degree, studying goats in the nearby Crazy Mountains. Tacked to a bulletin board in the university lab was a call for wildlife biologists needed in the territory of Alaska. As soon as the ink dried on Dad's diploma, he was packing his bags, eager to head north to the land of giant moose and grumpy grizzlies.

There were big plans in the young territory—talk of damming the Yukon, a river big enough to electrify the entire region. That first summer, Dad joined a three-man team floating the river's length to study the effects on fish and wildlife of a potential dam. A windstorm near the river's mouth swamped their flat-bottomed boat. Dad alone managed to climb atop the overturned hull, shivering and helpless in the middle of that wide river, figuring he was as good as dead until a man from a fish camp boated out and saved him. Whatever my father was thinking while watching steam lift from his soggy clothes strung up around that fish-camp fire, it didn't have anything to do with returning to Montana. If Alaska can kill you in a hundred different ways, it can, in a thousand more, make you feel more alive than you ever knew. Dad liked those odds.

In subsequent summers he observed the fisheries in Prince William Sound, counted caribou in the Nelchina Basin, and studied brown bears on the Alaska Peninsula. He accepted whatever job offer entailed getting to know some new wilder place. By the time I was born, a decade later, his fascination was focused on the life history of polar bears. My earliest memories are sculpted by the biting winds blowing off the sea ice into the village of Barrow where Dad worked at the Arctic Research Lab. I now know Barrow to be a place of edges, but as a child it was the center of my world. I assumed (if I thought about it at all) that every kid in the world rode to school on the back of a snow machine and had a wolfskin parka and sealskin boots. I had no concept of places where the sun came up all year round, where people strolled outside wearing indoor clothing. I had no idea there were towns, vast cities even, where whites outnumbered Eskimos.

When Dad's career ladder led to a position protecting wildlife from the effects of logging in Southeast Alaska, our family traded the frigid desert of the tundra for the soggy islands of the rainforest. Dad used the well-worn excuse of hunting as a means to explore the valleys and waterways surrounding our new Juneau home. As soon as I was old enough, I followed him through the woods. It started with afternoon hikes, Dad walking effortlessly through the devil's club and blueberries that dragged at my young body. Soon the hour-long outings grew into multiday expeditions. Annual hunts rolled into decades of tradition, eventually leading to a father crying with his son while digging for the scraps in an almost empty bag of trail mix.

Since leaving Montana, Dad's love for Alaska deepened like a finely aged marriage. It also opened him to the pain of progress. He witnessed four-wheeler trails cut through caribou calving grounds, remote valleys lost to yet another landing strip, trees scraped from quiet hillsides and sent to Japan, beaches and birds buried in oil. Dad studied polar bears for twenty years only to have them become the poster children for the ecological unraveling of the planet.

Dad allowed another tear, didn't try to wipe it away. His own sense of loss he could bear. The tears were for me, for the pain he knew would rise through my growing love. "It's like falling in love with a beautiful woman who is being abused and you can't do anything about it," he said as he stood and reached for his walking stick. "You're just forced to watch." He didn't mean to pass along the heartache—he just wanted to take his son hunting and share an alpine sunrise or two.

Dad winced as he put weight back on his stiffened knees. I watched him work down the steep hill until he disappeared behind the trees. I sat alone for a while. There was no hurry. I knew I would catch up.

Chapter Three

DOG OF GOD

WHILE CURLED TIGHTLY IN THEIR EGGS, most birds already know how to move through the world. Adult bar-tailed godwits, for example, nest in Alaska and then launch across the sea, abandoning their offspring on desolate beaches. Days later, the young birds open a map folded tightly into their DNA, point their bills across the Pacific, and follow. They fly a steady forty-five miles an hour, wings beating around the clock for almost a week. They track stars by night, the sun by day, and magnetic fields beneath cloudy skies. They cross the equator mid-trip, relying on their internal maps to make sense of the changing stars and the flip of the magnetic poles. The last of their fat reserves are gone as the rugged outline of New Zealand lifts above the horizon. After sixty-eight hundred miles they drop to a beach, take a long sip of water, tuck bill beneath wing, and sleep.

Young sandhills have no such sense of direction. Migration routes are learned from their parents rather than gleaned from chromosomes. Orphaned on the tundra, hatchlings stay put even as flocks of ducks, geese, and shorebirds stream south. They peck at the last of the insects in the growing cold before succumbing to the darkening days of the Arctic autumn. The absence of a genetic map, although lethal to the abandoned crane, may explain the longevity of the species. Since flight paths and stopovers are constantly taught, they can be quickly relearned.

The collective knowledge of any flock is repeatedly fine-tuned by the changing world under its wings.

Some cranes, through generations, have tightened migration routes, ultimately abandoning the annual movement altogether. Sandhills in Florida and Cuba, for example, stay put all year. Their young are taught the daily routes between riverside roost and grain-rich fields but learn nothing of the thousand-mile flights carrying the sandhills over Alaska.

Humans, like cranes, are both nomadic and sedentary, restless and rooted. Curled tightly in the womb, a fetus has no innate sense of when to travel or where to land. Each generation must learn anew how to move through the world.

———

I graduated from high school with no inherent idea of what to do next. All I knew was I wanted out of the building. Since the first grade, I'd felt confined by class, always eager for recess or the final bell. Each year the hallways seemed to narrow and the desks to tighten until, by my senior year, I felt imprisoned. When I turned eighteen I was able to excuse my own absences. I'd drop a note—*Please excuse Hank. He is sick.*—by the attendance office on my way to the ski hill. The attendance lady would eye my snow pants with suspicion but let me go. Maybe she knew school was my sickness, the outdoors my only cure.

I had no interest in another stack of textbooks, so while classmates compared colleges and conferred with guidance counselors I researched cheap tickets to faraway places. When I purchased passage to Bolivia I knew nothing of South America other than its distance from college campuses. After recovering from the graduation party, I tossed my diploma in a box and laid out enough clothes to get me through a year of traveling. Mom's tears at the airport startled me; my excitement for going didn't allow any room for the sadness of leaving.

The flight from Miami stopped in Panama and Venezuela before droning south through the night to La Paz. We landed in the early hours on an expansive, treeless plain stretched between distant snowy peaks. Following advice in my newly purchased traveler's handbook, I found my way to a hotel perched along a steep cobblestone street. I explored the frigid city for a few weeks, weaving through the bustling color of open-air markets and buying sizzling meat from nighttime vendors. When I met a Swiss man bound for the warmer climes of Cochabamba, I joined him for the all-night bus ride winding down steep mountain roads.

Unlike the precipitous layout of La Paz, the streets of Cochabamba stretched across the wide reach of a gentle valley. Palm trees grew along the main avenue. The air was thick, the sun warm. People moved slower and smiled more often than the folks scurrying beneath the chill in La Paz.

I eventually settled into a cheap hotel near the bus station. After a month on the road, the novelty of travel was wearing thin. I awoke each day with nothing to do. Eighty thousand people live in Cochabamba and I couldn't chat with any of them. If I could talk, I might have admitted the structure of high school looked pretty good compared to a world without language. Each morning I clicked the padlock shut on my room and walked the streets of Cochabamba, dictionary in hand, struggling to find the words for "ice cream" or "sandwich."

One day I noticed a nun surrounded by a gaggle of tattered children. Her Spanish was burdened by a thick American accent. I crossed the street and introduced myself. "It's lunchtime," she said. "Join us." I followed her into a rough-brick building where the throng of kids scrambled for chairs. The nun and I chatted above the boisterous boys and the clank of spoons scraping soup from cracked enamel bowls. I learned little about Sister Sarah other than she'd been in Bolivia for twenty years, dedicating each day to the never-ending task of housing and feeding the children of the streets. She didn't ask where I came from or how I got to Bolivia. Personal stories were incidental to the task at hand.

"What are you doing this afternoon?" she asked.

"No big plans."

"You got a good back?"

"Strong enough."

After lunch, she led me through the mess hall to an open courtyard where a three-man crew was laying the foundation for a new bunkhouse. I fell to work hauling bricks from the street to the courtyard, keeping each man supplied with a stack of the rough-hewn red blocks. I returned each day, mixing mortar and hauling more bricks while Sister Sarah fretted and barked orders at the workers. When she bustled beyond hearing, one of the bricklayers asked, *"La hermana es como un perro, no?"* He set another brick while I flipped through my dictionary. The sister is like a dog, no?

"Si, un Perro de Dios." Yes, a Dog of God.

The men laughed and I smiled, delighted with my first joke in a new language.

A few weeks later, bricks hauled and the walls raised, Sister Sarah took me on a bus ride to an understaffed orphanage at the edge of town. She introduced me to the director, spun on her heels, and left. The Dog of God never asked if I wanted to be there, never asked how long I planned to stay. There were hungry children all over the city and the day was already half gone. The Dog knew I'd be all right, knew the boys would be the perfect companions; they had nothing better to do than sit beneath a shade tree and teach a gringo to talk.

———

Weeks later, while helping one of the boys shovel out the pigpen, I thought of my high-school buddies reporting for freshman orientations. I chuckled at the contrast between those faraway class schedules and my new life in the Bolivian orphanage. A pain in my hand brought me back from my daydream. The shovel handle, fashioned that morning from a tree I'd hacked down with a machete, was working up a nasty blister where a knot rubbed my palm. In need of a diversion, I flicked a shovel full of dry dung onto the sandaled feet of the young boy working with me.

"*Qué pasa, gringo?*" Daniel shouted and dumped a load on my shoes. A few other boys trotted over to see what the laughter was about. They leaned against the low adobe wall, chuckling and joking as Daniel and I cleaned our way from one end of the pen to the other. Gordo the pig stood at his slop tray and ignored all the fuss.

Daniel was my best teacher. He was twelve, small for his age, with one deformed shoulder hunched up near his ear. In the mornings I joined him where he sat alone in the mess hall waiting for the daily piece of bread and cup of milk. He'd greet me with a shy grin.

"*Buenos días, hermano.*"

"*Qué tal, Daniel? Cómo estás?*"

"*Bien no más, hermano.*"

During the daily soccer games he watched from beneath a tree, a pronounced limp keeping him from running with the other boys. Sometimes I played ball, but most days I joined Daniel on the patch of worn ground beneath his tree. We'd chat for hours, Daniel deeply amused by a grown man unable to speak. Beneath that tree I became unabashed with my mistakes, happy to push myself just to hear my new friend laugh. He was endlessly patient with his corrections. In the shade, alongside the shouts and banter of a ballgame, I slowly learned to speak and Daniel slowly realized what it felt like to have a friend.

I wrote a long letter about life at the orphanage and addressed it to Judy, Anya's mother. Judy had championed and encouraged my travel plans; I knew she'd be happy to hear where I had landed. I shared stories of the boys and described the sacks of flour stacked alongside the broken oven, the neglected garden tools, the rusted showers, the scarcity of books, and the absence of pencils. Judy shared my letter with her congregation and neighbors, and within weeks a few thousand dollars of donated money was wired down.

The first purchase was an industrial-sized bread oven. With help from the older boys and cheers from the younger ones, we hauled the shiny appliance into the run-down kitchen. With buckets of fresh paint and dozens of brushes, we spruced up the mess hall and the bunkhouse, covering decades of grime and cracks beneath a layer of bright white. We bought a flock of chickens, repaired the toilets, and installed working showers. We built an outdoor oven of adobe brick and waited for Gordo to get more *gordo*.

After several months, I began to realize that while repairs were helpful, they were not healing. More than fresh paint and new chairs, more than sharp shovels and shiny hoes, the boys needed me to stay, to be some tall white substitute for the fathers they didn't have. But I didn't have the stamina, the staying power, or the dedication of the Dog. I couldn't resist the pull of home, the memory of seaside fog and the close comfort of rainforest trees.

The boys decided to serve up Gordo for my last meal. Gordo, of course, had gotten a lot bigger in the months since we built the oven. Not until the oven was hot and Gordo was dead, gutted, slathered in hot sauce, and covered with palm leaves did we realize the oven was too small. Laughing at the mistake, the boys took turns whittling the door with machetes. Chiseling at the opening would have been easier if the oven wasn't already hot—easier but not as fun.

The first stars were winking in the clear mountain air when we pulled Gordo from the oven and laid him on a table borrowed from the mess hall. Mouth-watering steam wafted into the night as the palm leaves were peeled away. We ate Gordo right there, standing around the still-warm stove in the growing evening chill. No plates, no forks—just one large knife and dozens of eager, greasy hands. There was plenty of cold Coke and hot meat for everyone. For most of those boys it was the first time the food had ever outlasted their appetite.

I left the next day after breakfast. The boys escorted me to the dirt road bordering their soccer field.

"*Que te vaya bien!*"

"*Ciao hermano.*"

"*Hasta luego.*"

Daniel alone followed me to where the dirt lane met the paved road into town. We stood together waiting for a bus to come take me away. I believed it when I told him I would write, that I'd be back, that maybe, even, he could come and visit. Daniel believed it too. We needed it to be true. Otherwise there was no way I could have pulled my arm off his shoulder, grabbed my pack, and stepped into the idling bus.

———

I rode a slow train through the high country of southern Peru, the first leg of a long journey I had planned up through South and Central America and back to the States. In Cuzco I caught a bus bound for the Peruvian coast. I smelled the sea before I saw it, my head thrust through an open window. I sucked lungful after lungful of familiar salt air. Not until I had drunk my fill did I realize how truly thirsty I'd become in the landlocked Andes.

I crossed the equator at night, nestled in the back of an old pickup bouncing along a rutted coastal road. After a year spent staring at the strange southern sky, the sight of the Big Dipper, upside down on the northern horizon, swelled my growing nostalgia into acute homesickness. The next morning I joined fellow travelers around a seaside fire. It was on that tropical beach—fresh fish on the grill, ripe bananas within easy reach, sunrise over the Pacific, the banter of foreign voices—that I abandoned my travel plans. I hung around paradise a few more days, body surfing and scavenging green coconuts, before heading inland to the nearest airport.

From Quito I called my sister, who bought me a plane ticket home. I cleared my way past the sniffing dogs and glaring officials at Miami's U.S. customs and boarded a flight across the continent to Alaska. My excitement was quickly tempered by a claustrophobic nervousness; big cowboy hats, big voices, big cars, big butts pushed from all sides. I felt suddenly compressed by America. Coconuts, seaside fires, shade trees, roasted pigs, and Daniel all felt like a fading dream.

In Juneau, I took a taxi from the airport to surprise my parents. They were just coming back from a morning walk when I pulled into the driveway. My mother kept touching me, not quite sure I was back or really all there. Like an excited puppy, I babbled, trying to tell them everything at once. My stories spilled out in a jumble of Spanish and English. They listened, beaming, happy to have their son back regardless of the language he spoke.

To celebrate, my parents took me to a nice restaurant. By the time the dessert tray rolled around I was no longer having a good time. My body had arrived in the land of eighteen-dollars-a-plate blackened salmon, but my mind lingered in the lucky-if-you-have-bread halls of the orphanage. While the pleasant clink of forks and conversation drifted from neighboring tables, my mind swam through images from another hemisphere. I thought of Daniel's story, his mother leaving him in the hospital, unable to feed yet another child. The boys at the orphanage were the lucky ones. I had passed others on the street each day. Children wearing clothes I would not keep for rags, kicking through piles of trash for food, sniffing gas-soaked cloth to pass the time. I had watched policemen grab those kids and burn their arms with cigarettes because beggars, they told me, leave a bad impression of their country.

I had seen the men those boys would turn into, stepping over them at night, slumped and sleeping in the gutters. While traveling I'd seen hundreds of acres of homes, propped-up pieces of tin and wilting cardboard, stretching round the outskirts of La Paz and Lima. Each windstorm tore them down. Each rainstorm piled shit and trash along the uphill side of the shacks. Dogs, cagey and thin, ate the human shit and then their own. I had witnessed the violence that grows from such poverty: *campesinos* marching through the city to protest the unaffordable price of bread, the predictable government response of nightsticks and tear gas. In South America I'd witnessed tragedy I was powerless to change. Dining with my parents in the dimly lit restaurant, I felt seated at the source of the injustice itself.

Confusion swirled through me in the following weeks, stirred by each visit to the starkly lit, overstuffed shelves of a grocery store and each passing of a manicured lawn. I struggled to fit simple adobe dwellings into the overbuilt expanse of my childhood home. Each day I became more of a stranger in my own town. After months of being homesick, I quickly became sick of home.

Not knowing what else to do, I enrolled in the state university. As I was packing for Fairbanks, my father came into my room with a few sheets of paper. "Your mother and I, with some help from your grandfather, have been putting some college money away over the years."

We sat together on my bed as Dad explained the columns of numbers—the amount invested in the various accounts, the percentages earned. After decades of saving and careful investment, this was Dad's big moment.

"I don't want it," I snapped. "Keep it. I don't want anything to do with it." I turned my back and stuffed clothes into my bag. I kept packing until I heard him leave.

I had a small scholarship. I would get by with that. But refusing my parent's generosity did nothing to ease my guilt. Standing in line to pay for books and classes, I thought about how much bread my tuition could buy. Through lectures, drunken freshman parties, ping-pong tournaments, and basketball games, I thought about the one torn soccer ball shared by all those boys in Cochabamba. By day, I studied the chemical pathways of photosynthesis and the molecular structures of sugars. By night, I drank beer with gusto, pretending to be part of the crowd.

———

Between one wetland refuge and the next, cranes may battle headwinds and low clouds. Young birds keep in tight formation, trusting whoever is at the head of the V to find the way. Returning from South America, I was buffeted by guilt. Each place I tried to land was obscured by the dark stain of my own anger. I was alone, isolated from the contentment of friends and family. By Christmas, I could do it no more. I dropped out of the university. I returned home and rattled around my parents' house for a few weeks and then called Frank to ask if his cabin was available.

"No plans for it. It's all yours," Frank said.

I borrowed Dad's skiff and made the cold run to the island. Unlike the last icy trip with Frank at the helm, the water was flat. I hauled boxes of food into the cabin, stoked the stove, unrolled my sleeping bag. When night fell I sat alone, the hiss of the gas lantern and an avalanche of thoughts my only company.

I spent daylight hours walking the frozen beaches or creeping through the cold woods. The long nights confined me to the tiny cabin. Pen as shovel, I dug through my confusion. Each night the plywood table grew more cluttered with pages of rambling prose. I realized that I couldn't go back, Bolivia could never be my home: I'd always be the stranger, the gangly gringo, no matter how fluent my Spanish. How then could I stay?

What use were memories of poverty in a land of riches? Where, in an unjust world, could I build a home?

A week, maybe ten days into my time on the island, I found myself singing. Not booming glorious songs, just little ditties while I hopped between beach stones or watched ducks feeding at sunset. The isolation I felt in the crowded dorm and bustling cafeteria eased in the quiet forest. The trees did not expect me to fit in. They did not care about my questions, did not pretend any answers. They stood with steady indifference through quiet and gale, moonlight and snowfall; the perfect response for a mind drowning in drama. With each passing day, I felt a little less guilty, a little more human.

After several weeks I was ready for conversation, ready for company other than the babbling ducks, quiet trees, and elusive deer. The night before I left, I collected the pages of scrawled thoughts from the table and stuffed them into an envelope. I wrote Anya's name on the front. We had not seen each other since that cold hunt two years earlier. She was, her parents told me, in Germany, studying at the University of Tübingen. On the back of the envelope I wrote that I wasn't sure why I was shipping the avalanche her way. But I felt some vague comfort imagining her holding my story on the other side of the world.

I skiffed back to town on a flat, calm day. My spirits skimmed like the aluminum hull over the surface of the sea. In the final mile before the boat harbor, I streamed through a hail storm, laughing above the whine of the outboard as the pellets stung my face.

Chapter Four

DEATH OF A TRAVEL BUG

ALTHOUGH GREGARIOUS IN MIGRATION, sandhill cranes are fiercely solitary while nesting. Mated pairs drive intruding cranes from their breeding territory with flying lunges and jabbing bills. The chicks hatch beneath their parents' protective stance. Colts are precocious, scrabbling about within days, lurching after insects, and then burrowing into the safe warmth of their parents' feathers when they need a rest. They grow fast, doubling their body weight every few days. Eight weeks from the egg, they experiment with short soaring flights, strengthening their wings for the long journey ahead.

In the shortening days of August, the family flies off and joins other cranes in a lakeside marsh or river floodplain. In those staging areas, the young cranes stay close to their parents but listen intently to the growing clatter of voices. As the journey south continues, they're joined by still more cranes, rivulets of birds coalescing along a river of memory. Weeks later, settling into California cornfields or Mexican marshes, the juvenile birds are comfortable within the cacophonous chorus. Carried by collective experience, the colts are taught to roost in rice paddies or river bends at night and lift over freeways and skirt the rows of condos by day. The bonds with parents weaken as their ease with the flock gains strength. Buoyed by the mentorship of many, the adolescent cranes learn how to navigate the edge of suburbia.

Returning from my own migration across the hemispheres, I found myself, like the California cranes, negotiating edges, searching for a calm place to land. The dorm was too crowded, the solitude of Frank's cabin too lonely, the clamor in a city too chaotic. I met few people charting a course I was drawn to follow.

From the sea of possible mentors, two men rose tall. One lived in the rich damp of an Alaskan rainforest, the other in the bleak cold of the Bolivian Andes. One spoke English, the other Aymaran. One held a master's degree in comparative anatomy, the other had never been to school. Although living in separate hemispheres, both men went to sleep at night with dark bits of earth packed beneath their fingernails; both lived in simple homes built with their own hands; both harvested a deep satisfaction along with a large crop of potatoes.

―――

Most of us are completely blind to the patterns Greg Streveler perceives every time he steps off his porch. The way a bear filters the rich kaleidoscope of scents wafting through its nose or a deer amplifies tiny sounds by shifting its ears, Greg had honed an understanding of the world beyond normal human senses. Greg began absorbing patterns and paw prints the moment he arrived in Gustavus as a new biologist with the National Park Service. Thirty years later, he is a living archive of insights. In fresh snow or soft mud he can, with a quick glance, decipher the tiny prints of voles from the still tinier tracks of shrews. From a tide-line bone fragment, his mind's eye reconstructs an entire skeleton complete with evolutionary history. Give him an afternoon in the woods with a shovel and tree corer, and he'll tell you where sea level was three hundred years ago. Where most of us see a static assemblage of plants, Greg intuits a landscape flowing through time.

Along with his keen curiosity, Greg arrived from his native Wisconsin with a crate of hand tools. He bought timbers from a local sawyer and a chunk of ground from a neighboring homesteader. With a farm boy's hard work and a young man's passion, he crafted a home in a stand of young pine. Beneath dim kerosene lights in that simple cabin, he raised two children. He hauled kelp from the beach and enriched a plot of ground. Rather than push a cart through supermarket aisles, he worked a hoe between the rows of his garden. Rather than fill an account with cash, he stuffed a root cellar with spuds and beets. As he carved a life in the young land, the land cut back, shaping the life of the young man.

On my first trip to Gustavus, I didn't meet Greg or anyone else on the deserted roads. I came as a student on a high-school field trip. This wasn't a board-the-yellow-bus-for-the-afternoon type of outing. My biology teacher loaded a couple dozen students on a boat for a ten-day exploration of Glacier Bay. On the way back to Juneau, Mr. Jurasz had the boat stop at the long Gustavus pier so his cooped-up students could blow off some steam. It was May, sunny. The perfume of new cottonwood leaves saturated the air. I joined my band of boisterous friends pouring down the quiet dirt roads. In five hours we saw four people and three cars. The town had one scantily stocked general store, a tiny lumberyard open two days a week, and a gas pump open every Saturday afternoon.

After that introduction I wanted more. The summer between my junior and senior years of high school, I volunteered for the National Park Service in Gustavus, flying the sixty miles from Juneau in a single-engine air taxi. The pilot pulled up alongside a tiny A-frame office, one of two structures bordering the lonely runway. When I stepped from the plane, bird song mixed with the tick of the cooling engine. My supervisor for the summer met my flight. We rattled down ten miles of dusty road in a government truck to Park Headquarters where I was given a tiny room in a musty trailer dubbed Toad Hall.

Although Greg no longer worked for the Park Service, he was the go-to guy when someone spotted a bizarre bird or found an oddball plant. He'd show up at the office, identify the bird, and key out the specimen. After answering our queries, he'd ask his own. Had anyone seen the golden eagle at the kittiwake colony this year? How many sea lions were hauled out on North Marble Island? How about coyote tracks in the Beardslee Islands? His appetite for information was endless. Questions were his tools for deepening his relationship to his home.

When Greg offered the bunk in his tiny guest cabin, I gladly gathered my gear from Toad Hall. When he offered a plot of ground in his fertile garden, I picked up a shovel and went to work. I quickly realized Greg was a master in the art of making do. His home was sided with scavenged shingles, his bike was built from an amalgam of discarded parts, his shovel handle shaped from the trunk of a young spruce, his kayak a patched wreckage pulled from the tide.

As well as welcoming me into his home, Greg invited me into the landscape. Pulling bugs from a willow tree, he showed me the difference between a beetle and a weevil. While weeding the garden, he'd pause to point out the subtle distinction between a junco's trill and an orange-crowned warbler's chatter. But for every easy answer Greg peppered me with a dozen hard questions. "Look at this," he said, poking his walking stick into a moss-covered log. "It's bigger than any of the trees in this forest. Where did this log come from? How did it get here?"

"No clue," I said.

"Well, think about it. I'll bet you'll figure it out by the end of summer."

On another forest hike, he pointed out the absence of young pine trees. "Why do you think these trees are not reproducing?" Greg asked. "What is the forest going to look like in fifty years?" I shrugged, both embarrassed by all that I did not see and excited at the chance to sharpen my sight.

We made a tight pair that summer, a man eager to teach and a kid hungry to learn. Greg took me trolling when the cohos ran thick. He coached me through filleting, brining, and smoking the rich red meat. He fed me meals of baked cod and fried spuds. He loaned me a chainsaw and split-ting maul to fill the shed alongside the cabin. I was grateful for the atten-tion and Greg seemed glad for the company. He saw in me who he used to be and I saw in him what I might someday become.

———

Uramuro was Aymaran Indian, a full twelve inches shorter than me and twice as thick through the chest. His last name I couldn't pronounce. I never saw it written. He didn't own a pencil, not sure he could use it if he did. Years of intense mountain sun had carved deep creases across his face. Crude sandals made from strips of discarded tires wrapped his cracked and calloused feet. Hand-stitched patches covered his worn clothes. He was in his thirties but looked older—fifty, maybe sixty.

He avoided the crush of poverty in the nearby cities by staying where he was born—an adobe hut exposed to the steady altiplano winds. He tilled the rocky soil of his parents' fields with a hand-carved plow yoked between two mismatched cows. His younger children shepherded a ragged flock of sheep across the barren valley.

Uramuro's brother, whom I met in Cochabamba, arranged my visit. With directions tucked into my shirt pocket, I told Daniel and the other boys at the orphanage I'd be back in few weeks. I boarded the miniature bus for the long ride up to La Paz, where I switched to an equally uncom-fortable bus that sputtered and climbed out of the city's jumble and then across the flat expanse of the altiplano. Muted browns gave way to the jagged white brilliance of eighteen-thousand-foot peaks. Small adobe buildings peppered the stark valley.

After a few hours, the bus stopped for a man waving his arms by the roadside. We introduced ourselves as the bus grumbled away. Uramuro led me along a faint trail stretching away from the road. It was Novem-ber, springtime in the southern mountains. Bright green shoots poked through the brittle brown of last year's grass. We visited a dozen homes along the path. Families came out to gawk at the skinny white giant. I winked and smiled at children peering from between their parents' legs.

Uramuro's home, like the others, was fashioned of roughly formed adobe bricks. Twenty filthy, matted sheep were pinned against one end of the house by a three-foot-high mud fence. The doorway on the main house barely reached my chin (an endless source of amusement for the children). Shafts of sun beamed through the two small window openings. The steady altiplano wind whispered through the house and covered everything with a fine grit. Three beds made of adobe bricks were heaped with sheepskins that smelled strongly of their former owners. Seven people shared the space: Uramuro, his wife, their three youngest children, and Uramuro's brother and sister-in-law. They gave me a bed all to myself. The rest slept like stacked logs.

The kitchen had a separate entrance at the back of the house. We gathered there each morning and evening, sitting on the skin-covered floor as the mother fed dried cow dung into a tiny adobe oven. There was no chimney, just a hole in a corner of the roof. The room filled with acrid, eye-stinging smoke. The meals centered around one of many varieties of potatoes: watery potato soup with guinea pig legs, sheep cheese crumbled onto a plate of boiled and diced potatoes, finger-like potatoes dipped into a bowl of mashed potatoes. Lunch, which we ate in the fields, was boiled potatoes (wrapped in a blanket and still warm from the morning fire) and crumbly cheese.

When not busy eating potatoes, I assisted in the planting of them. I did my best to suck enough oxygen from the thin mountain air to keep up with the barrel-chested Uramuro. With gentle clicks and clucks, he coaxed the two black cows pulling a hand-hewn wooden plow. One of the daughters followed behind and dropped in the seed potatoes. My job was simple: scoop powdery cow dung into a blanket and sprinkle it down each row like pouring flour from a huge sack. Every day at lunch, my oxygen-starved brain gave out and I would wake to find my companions already back at work, snickering at the lazy gringo.

On rare nights when I was still awake after dinner, I huddled with the others around the meek flame of a candle as we stuttered through stories of our lives. I shared pictures of my home: polar bears and sea ice, whales and bears, my school, my house. What impressed them most were houses made of wood. Of the seven people pressed around those photos, only Umaruro had traveled far enough to see a tree. He told of the long trip to Lake Titicaca and the tall swaying branches growing at the water's edge.

Uramuro said he would like to visit me one day. He asked about airplane rides. What is it like to leave the earth? He laughed when he heard the price of a ticket. He ran the numbers and figured he could almost afford the trip if he sold both his cows, his sheep, his plow, his bicycle. Uramuro laughed again as the insanity sank deeper and then casually, yet with great sincerity, shared a thought that has traveled with me through all the years and miles that separate me from those clear nights. He said he could not imagine a happier life than the one he was living. He had everything he needed and desired—shelter, food, and a family to share it with. His days held no questions. He yearned for and lacked nothing. He knew where he lived and where he would die.

I had dreams of being a world traveler, but Uramuro's words struck a gentle yet lethal blow to my travel bug. It wasn't an epiphany really. No flashing lights, blaring horns, or singing angels. I didn't repent and swear to never travel again. But when I returned home, I put my passport in a safe place and never thought about it again. Although it was slow to take root, Uramuro planted the idea that moving would keep me from ever finding the contentment under my feet.

Chapter Five

COLOR CHANGE

FRANK WASN'T SEARCHING. Like Greg and Uramuro, he was rooted in place. There were questions in his life, but where to spend his days was not one of them. The tight orbit between his house, woodshed, funky old office, and hunting cabin was all the space he needed. He'd briefly leave the yard most days, lacing up his running shoes to train for his annual marathon. He hopped in and out of the roadside ditch as he ran, picking up trash, returning home sweaty, happy, hands filled with crushed beer cans.

Taped to his office wall was a Garrison Keillor quote: *Some luck lies in not getting what you thought you wanted, but getting what you have, which, once you have it, you may be smart enough to see is what you would have wanted had you known.* There were buckets of bent nails on the porch waiting to be straightened. The woodshed was built from creosote timbers from a collapsed dock. The potbelly stove in his office came from the dump, the windows from an old mining building. The house was spiked together with wave-worn boards brought in by the tide. The paneling in the stairwell, silvered with age, came from an old cannery. In a culture obsessed with more, Frank was content with what came his way. He was smart enough to know how lucky he was.

Rooted by the sea, Frank was an anchor. Anya's sisters and foster brother, Joe, worked across town, across the state, or across the world, tethered to Frank's steady weight. It was easy to leave knowing he was there: house warm, cookies fresh, teapot ready.

Of all his children, Anya most keenly shared Frank's passion for berries and deer. On the mountain she was his faithful scout, in the berry patch his steady companion. When schooling kept Anya from the mountain, Frank sent the hunt to her. In long letters, he detailed the boat ride, the hike, each stretch of forest, every deer seen, who else went, what they said. Along with the words he sent jars of jam and packages of backstrap—food vital to the woman he was helping his daughter become.

After my solo time at Frank's cabin, I kicked around my parents' house for a few months before applying to Evergreen State College, a funky liberal arts school in Olympia, Washington. If a typical university didn't fit, maybe there'd be room for me at a school with no grades and no required courses. Before leaving for college, I drove out to Frank's place to say goodbye. When he saw me coming across the yard he smiled, set down his pencil, and pulled open the door.

"There are just a few cookies left," he said. "We'd better eat 'em before they get stale." Frank brewed a patch of coffee. We brought the cookies and our steaming cups to the dining room table overlooking the cove. The tide was high. A half dozen harlequin ducks darted and dove through a gentle north sea lapping the rocks below us.

"Have you found a place to live down there?" Frank asked.

"Nope, not yet."

"You know what you're going to study?"

"Nope, got to figure that out too."

"Hey!" Frank exclaimed. "Anya came back from Germany last week. She's starting classes in Seattle. Maybe you two can get together sometime." He scratched a phone number on a scrap of paper and pushed it across the table.

"Thanks," I said, pocketing the paper and reaching for another cookie. I turned, pretending to be absorbed in watching the ducks, delaying my departure from the welcoming warmth of Frank's home.

A few days later, after registering for classes, I rechecked the campus housing board in search of a room. There were scraps of paper several layers deep with invitations to join about every living situation imaginable and a few that were not. Vegetarian homes were the norm; deviations such as wheat-free or dairy-free were boldly noted. A few, oddly enough, even claimed to be drug-free. Beside culinary orientation, there was a strong sexual bias across the board. Nowhere was there an invitation tailored to me—a straight, white, new-age redneck male with a hankering for a forty-eight-ounce butt roast.

I copied addresses and made the rounds, failing one interview after another. It was late afternoon when I pedaled up to the last place on my list: a rambling old farmhouse sunk into an overgrown yard on a dead-end street. The matriarch of the house looked like Janis Joplin reincarnate. She invited me in.

"Just fixing breakfast," she said, offering no apologies that it was almost dinnertime. "You care for a spirulina smoothie?"

"Spirulina?"

"Yeah, you know. Algae. The lowest rung on the food chain. You are a vegetarian, aren't you?"

Caught between honesty and homelessness, I lied.

"Of course. I never eat meat."

"Great," said Ms. Joplin, handing me a tall glass of thick green goo. "There's one spot left. Let me show it to you."

I followed Janis up two flights of stairs to a tight room with sloping ceilings. An aggressive black mold crept from the dark corners. A flock of fruit flies hovered near the only window.

"Perfect. I'll take it."

While unpacking, I found Frank's scrap of paper. I called Anya from the downstairs phone. She seemed happy to learn I was close by and she eagerly accepted my invitation to visit. The next weekend she braved the high speeds of Interstate 5. Her long black hair was now cropped tight to her head, but her wide smile had not changed at all. Up in my room she pulled out two packages wrapped in white butcher paper. On each one, in her father's neat block letters, were the words: BACKSTRAP—ADMIRALTY.

We waited until nearly midnight. I cracked the door, poked my head into the hallway, and listened. The house was still. "I think everyone's asleep. Let's go." We eased down the creaky attic steps to the kitchen. Anya sliced the venison into small round steaks while I diced an onion and heated a skillet. The sizzling pop of hot grease soon filled the kitchen. "I'll bet they'll be able to smell it in the morning," I whispered.

"Do you think they'd really kick you out?" Anya asked.

"Not sure. They are definitely dedicated vegetarians and I did lie to them."

We stacked the steaming meat onto a plate, gave the skillet a quick scrub, and carried our treasure back upstairs. Other than a beanbag and a worn-out futon, there was no furniture in the room. We lit a candle, sat on the lumpy mattress, and fed each other hot bites of meat with our fingers.

"Not the most balanced meal," Anya said, licking her fingers. "We could have cooked a vegetable."

"Onions are vegetables."

"I meant a green vegetable."

"We'll buy green onions next time."

Balanced or not, we ate it all, over a pound of meat apiece. We blew out the candle and curled up on the narrow futon. Sealed with a greasy kiss, our romance took root in that old house filled with industrious mice and militant algae eaters.

We saw each other every weekend after that. Anya was renting a room in a seventh-floor apartment on Seattle's bustling University Way—fifty miles and a world away from the hippie haven of Evergreen. The patchouli oil and dreadlocks at my campus were countered by Old Spice and crew cuts at U of W. I journeyed between those worlds in a 1962 Volvo that burned a quart of oil with each weekly round-trip.

Every Friday, I'd wait until after rush hour to make the drive, hugging the freeway shoulder so I'd have a place to coast to a stop when the Volvo choked on its own black exhaust. Arriving in the U District in late evening, just as the frat parties were gearing up, I'd cruise narrow streets dominated by Phi Kappa This and Delta Alpha That, looking for a place to park. After easing my beater in between some shiny cruisers, I'd walk past blocks of weekend revelers hanging from windows or dancing on lawns to find Anya waiting in her apartment.

She shared her place with Charlotte, an eighty-year-old deaf woman who beamed in vicarious enjoyment of our new romance. A staunch proponent of fresh air, Charlotte kept the heat on high and the windows opened wide. She was, of course, blissfully unaware of the sounds that blew in with the breeze. While Charlotte snored in the next room, Anya and I lay in bed and listened to the nutcase on the street corner below screaming scriptures and preaching hellfire.

In an odd way I feel indebted to that frenetic freeway and ranting preacher, to those puking partiers and vehement vegetarians. Had our romance begun in the familiar calm of the rainforest, we might not have held each other so tight. Amid the clamor and lights we found refuge in our shared love for the quiet gray skies of home. Sleeping seven stories above that bustling street the world I missed fit perfectly in my arms.

———

During our weekends together, Anya would read the latest of Frank's letters out loud to me. Although a thousand miles away, we tagged along on the hunt—bouncing through the boat ride, imagining the cabin's warmth and lantern's shadows, visualizing the sudden appearance of deer and the familiar faces of the other hunters.

Over a meal of backstrap in Charlotte's tiny kitchen, Anya told me she wouldn't be able to be in the city if Frank were not at home tending to the garden and berry patches. "I can only be here because I know he is there."

For Anya, Frank was an anchor. For me, he was a magnet. Opposites attract. His contentment was a powerful counter to my confusion. He seemed integral to the beach, as much a part of the cove as the rye grass or red alder trees towering over his office. Reading and rereading his letters in Charlotte's apartment, I thought Frank would always be there, that I'd have plenty of time to see through the eyes of a man not looking for more. Anya never dreamed she'd already made the last climb with her father.

I was back in Olympia when the call came. I stumbled through dreams down the steep stairs to the ringing phone. Although half asleep, I instantly recognized the shift in Judy's voice.

"All I know," Judy said, "is that he lived the way he wanted to."

I drove my Volvo up I-5. Frat row was quiet, plenty of parking spaces. Anya opened the door, looking pale and taut, eyes red.

"The colors have all changed," Anya said as she collapsed in my arms. "They have all gone flat."

We joined up with Anya's older sister, Frith, and caught the next flight north, riding an almost empty plane through a tear-filled night. In Juneau, Judy, Anya's other sister, Mihkel, and Frank's best friend, Steve Jacoby, were there to embrace us. "He was my guiding light," Steve whispered as we hugged. "What do you do when you lose your light?"

Bit by bit we heard the story. Frank's truck was in the driveway, but he wasn't in his office when Mihkel came home in the afternoon. His boots were not on the porch. His float suit was not on the peg. By dinnertime the neighbors were called.

"Yeah," Larry said, "he borrowed my rowboat around two o'clock to pull the crab pot. I just checked. The boat is not back."

It was cold, early December. Full moon, the first of two that month. With flashlights, the search began. Friends and neighbors walked the beaches and probed between boulders. They scanned their brains for a story that would have him alive.

By ten o'clock a Coast Guard boat motored into the cove. Steve climbed into their inflatable to help search. The spotlight showed nothing but tight waves on a black sea. Around midnight they checked the crab pot. Steve was hauling the line when the body lifted into view. He cut his friend loose from the tangle of rope and rolled him aboard. On shore, Steve did mouth to mouth, offering his breath to reverse the impossible. He didn't quit until the ambulance came. The medics loaded up Frank's body. The lights, flashing with urgency on arrival, were still as the ambulance pulled up the driveway.

At the funeral I looked back from the front pew at a jammed church. A sea of friends and neighbors spilled into the lobby, back into the kitchen, and out onto the sidewalk. If you didn't know Frank, you were new to town. Frank was born in Juneau. His father, a German immigrant, was a carpenter. His uncle was a local dairy farmer. As a kid, Frank won the Soap Box Derby and made headlines boarding a prop plane to represent Alaska in the national competition in Ohio. With ruler and pencil, he designed new homes, remodeled old ones. With placards and signs, he defended trees, protested wars. With grit and a smile, he ran races and won volleyball championships. He baked pies three at time, one to eat hot, one to eat cold, and one to give away.

But his greatest work was done with hot drinks and fresh cookies. Following the service, stories of tea with Frank circled around the church. I never thought the attention he gave me was a gift offered to anyone who knocked on his door. But the stories kept coming: Frank the confidant;

Frank the neighbor; Frank the man who was always there; Frank the guy who gave his time as if he had more than he needed. Had things been different, had someone else been pulled from their boat, it would have been Frank who, one by one, helped us make sense of the loss.

After the funeral we returned to Seattle, where Anya faced a week of final exams. She floated through student life like a ghost, everything familiar suddenly foreign. Her anchor gone, Anya drifted. There was little she could do beyond the daily work of carrying the weight of sadness.

———

It was Anya who knew what to do with the ashes. Frank had told her, years earlier, as they sat shoulder to shoulder on an alpine ridge. Somewhere up here, he said. Sprinkle them in the deer cabbage.

His daughters, his wife, and a few hunting companions made the trip. We boated to the cabin in July, the wind warm, the seas calm. We took turns carrying the simple pine box up the mountain. Above tree line, the shady side of the ridge was still pinned beneath dense patches of snow. Anya kicked steps into the icy snow, leading us to the place where she'd sat so many times with her dad. We gathered on the ridge top, sucking on snowballs to cool ourselves after the long climb. Someone pried the lid loose and laughed. Nestled atop Frank's ashes were a few cookies—butterscotch oatmeal.

We spread the ashes slowly, mixing them with prayers and tears. Anya scooped a handful and carried them to the edge of a cliff. As she tossed her father's bones, a puff of wind, like breath on a cold day, blew a gray mist back into her long black hair.

In all the years Anya followed her father up that hill, she never carried a gun. She was content with her binoculars, happy to let her dad do the shooting. Late that night, curled tight in sleeping bags, Anya whispered that she needed to learn to hunt. If the sea could take her father, Anya explained, it could take me, Richard, any of the hunters in her life. The only way to ensure a steady supply of venison was to gather it herself.

"Not much good scouting without a hunter," Anya said.

I wanted to say I'd always be there. Wanted to say I was glad to have her as my scout. But with the residue of Frank's ashes still on our hands there was no point in empty promises.

"Reckon not," I said.

"Will you teach me how to shoot?" Anya asked.

"Of course."

We climbed the mountain a month later for our annual hunt. Before we headed up the hill, Anya spent a few hours on the beach practicing with Frank's rifle. The gun was too heavy. The recoil too sharp. The loss too fresh. Anya wiped her tears so she could see through the scope and kept shooting.

We awoke the next morning on the summit. Three-thirty and the rising sun already tickled the eastern sky. We ate a cold breakfast while waiting for the earth to spin its way into daylight. Clouds on fire, murrelets whistling over the ridge, Anya and I set off together, creeping into the saddle between our camp knob and the high reach of the main peak. Always the impatient one, I wandered back and forth, peering into side bowls while Anya crept along, spending long minutes standing and watching.

Anya was alone when a large buck walked into the opening in front of her. The deer stopped and watched as Anya rested her father's gun on the twisted branch of a mountain hemlock. The deer fell a few feet from an alpine pond. By the time I got there, Anya was kneeling by the animal, hand on its side. On the pond's surface floated a single white feather from the tail of a bald eagle.

We broke camp around midday and loaded our packs for the long climb down. Before leaving the ridge top, Anya went to the cliff edge where she'd tossed her father's ashes. She stood there a long time, meat heavy in her pack, rifle on her shoulder. I don't know what she said, what she was thinking. I left her alone. Whatever she was looking for at the edge of the rock I could not help her find.

I don't remember what we called the mountain while Frank was still alive. Doesn't really matter. We call it Frank's Mountain now. Anya wants her ashes spread up there in the deer cabbage. I wonder what we'll call the mountain then.

Chapter Six

SAWDUST AND CRANES

ANYA NEVER IMAGINED HERSELF IN A HOSPITAL, stethoscope around her neck, prescription pad in her pocket. She started college as a drama major, dreaming of theaters and scripts, curtain calls and bright lights. But everything changed when a friend from her freshman acting class enticed her to take an evening course in midwifery. After witnessing her first birth, Anya knew the power of the stage was no match for the magic of the delivery room. She switched to nursing, the quickest path into the world of babies. A few years before he died, Frank told his daughter that she didn't have to be a nurse, that she could give the orders rather than take them. Before those words of encouragement, Anya had never contemplated life as a doctor.

We both knew that medical school, followed by residency, would launch Anya on a seven-year journey a thousand miles from the Alaska she loved. "I'll apply to one school," Anya said. "If they don't take me, I'll come home." While Anya worked on that application, I put in for a job with the National Park Service at Glacier Bay. The letters came back within a week of each other. We both got what we asked for. Sitting together in my attic bedroom beneath the lazy flock of fruit flies, it did not feel like good news.

I finished my last class and left town before the diplomas were handed out. I sold the old Volvo to a housemate for the price of a ride to the Seattle airport. We swung by to pick up Anya who was sitting on her luggage on the sidewalk beneath her apartment building. Outside the Alaska Airlines entrance, I watched, without a trace of nostalgia, as my car sputtered off in front of its black cloud.

With three months before Anya's school and my work pulled us apart, we moved into Greg's little Gustavus cabin, cooking our meals over a one-burner camping stove set up on the tiny covered porch. We both landed summer work smoking salmon and packaging halibut for a local fish processor. Evenings, we weeded, pruned, and admired our miniature garden growing next to Greg's extensive jungle. Weekends, we borrowed kayaks and explored the maze of islands in the lower reaches of Glacier Bay. Nestled in our nylon tent, we listened for snuffling bears and fell asleep to the flutelike song of hermit thrushes.

One day we found a baby crow, featherless and red, on the ground. Anya scooped the starving bird to her chest and carried it back to the cabin. She made a moss-lined nest near the head of our bed and fell to the steady task of stuffing food down the gaping mouth. Its feathers grew along with its appetite and soon it was hopping about the house and yard screaming for more grub. Our crow didn't have a name until he learned to fly and took off with our pencils, spoons, sunglasses, or anything else that fit in his devious beak. We called him Diablo after that.

I was just twenty-three that summer, obsessed with finding in the forested seaside town a piece of contentment I'd glimpsed in the treeless Bolivian mountains. Although settled in Gustavus, I was still running, fleeing from the obscenity of consumerism, moving too fast to find any satisfaction. I didn't know Uramuro's contentment was born of still feet and calm mind. I believed all I needed was my own piece of land, enough acres to keep encroachment at bay. If I couldn't stop the industrial revolution from ravaging the continent, then I'd step aside and let it roll on by. If modern living was running humanity toward a cliff, then I saw no reason to get in the way.

In all my anger, I believed all I needed was a garden, root cellar, and woodstove, and I'd have no need for promised comforts. Once my home was built I'd sit back and watch the oil spigots run dry and commerce grind to a halt. Let the luxury of Chilean grapes and New Zealand apples be torn from hands too soft to work the earth. Let the rich run shivering from their opulent mansions when the furnaces gasp and sputter their last breaths. Just give me a little cabin in the woods and I'd shake myself free of the injustice of the American dream.

Anya might have traded hospital corridors for the rows of our own garden; she might have let go of her plans to be a part of mine, might have stayed if I asked. But I didn't. I was too young, too consumed with my own well-being to truly make room for anyone else. Blinded by the illusion that the safest refuge was built with walls of solitude, I let her go.

The day before Anya left for school a goshawk snatched our pet from the air. The hawk landed with our squawking crow in the far corner of the garden. When the hawk repositioned his grip and took off again, Diablo was silent.

———

Small towns get smaller in winter. With tourists gone, each fresh face becomes a possible neighbor. At the post office one day I held the door for a stout, slow-moving man. He thanked me before asking what I was doing in town. As we checked our boxes I explained that I was looking to build a home. He smiled as though he'd heard the story a hundred times. Chatting in the warmth of the post office, I learned that Gary Owen lived alone on a one hundred forty-acre homestead on the north end of town. After decades of having the place all to himself he had decided to punch in a roadway, sell off some parcels, and create a bit of a neighborhood.

"You know how to run a saw?" Gary asked.

"Sure," I lied.

"Stop by my place this spring. We'll get the logging done, then mill up some boards. You can have all the two-by-sixes you want."

When I showed up in early May, Gary seemed surprised. He invited me in and reheated a batch of weak coffee. I reminded him of our midwinter conversation. By the bottom of Gary's third cup, the faraway commitment to work together slowly came into focus.

"Come back tomorrow and we'll get started," Gary said. I arrived early, primed for work. In contrast to my eagerness, Gary moved at a pace honed by a life of physical labor. I fidgeted about as Gary patiently sharpened the saw and greased the excavator. It was midmorning before we were positioned at the start of the new road.

"Just lay 'em all down next to each other pointed back my way," Gary explained. "Limb the big ones and buck 'em at sixteen feet. I'll sort 'em with the machine. The road is sixty feet wide. Keep it straight. Don't want the thing winding all over the goddamn place."

"Sure thing," I responded, hefting the chainsaw with the contrived confidence of a wannabe logger. A few quick pulls and the saw snarled to life. I chose a spindly pine to start. Gary watched from the cab of the excavator as the tree fell perpendicular to the roadway and hung up in nearby branches. He climbed down, half smiling.

"Give me that thing. Let me show you something before you kill yourself."

Gary stepped up to a large spruce, cut a deep V open to the direction of the intended fall, then back-cut it from the opposite side. The tree fell like an obedient dog. Gary dropped several more and began limbing. I stretched a tape along each denuded trunk as Gary cut them to length.

The sap was running thick with the pull of spring. In the following days, I dropped hundreds of trees. Some of them even fell the right way. A thin mist of sticky pitch spun from the saw's teeth and blackened my shirt and gloves. Wood chips found their way under my collar and down my boots. While I sweated, Gary sat placidly in the excavator, fingertips on the controls, toothpick dangling from his lips.

After a week, I no longer watched them drop. I'd look up, note the direction of fall, and then sink the saw's teeth in the next tree before the previous one hit the ground. We worked long days, stopping only to refuel the saw and gobble a sandwich. During a lunch break Gary paused between bites to share a bit of philosophy.

"All these goddamn tree huggers not wanting to cut nothing. Well, it's all a bunch of *bowlll shit.*" Emphasis was always on the "bowl," pronounced in four distinct syllables with a strong explosive *b.* "Every goddamn one of 'em is living in a wooden house wiping their ass with a tree."

Gary's words were a jab at me, a practical man's poke at a young man's idealism. He was amused to watch me use hydraulics and saws to level a forest to make boards to build a refuge from modern society. He smiled to see my excitement for home trailed by a long shadow of guilt. Gary bit into his sandwich and watched me squirm.

After two weeks, the cutting was done: a straight, half-mile canyon slashed through the woods. The intricacy of forest was gone. In its place was raw earth stamped by the track of a machine, a cavernous testimonial to technology and intention. A sense of accomplishment outweighed any feelings of regret.

"Another couple weeks cutting and you could pass for a logger," Gary chided.

"Another couple weeks and there wouldn't be anything left to log," I responded.

We trucked the logs to Gary's mill and rolled the first one in place alongside the huge circular blade. Gary sharpened the hooked teeth and oiled the old engine. I fidgeted.

"You got a cut list?" Gary asked.

"Cut list?"

"Let's take a look at your house plans."

"House plans?"

Gary smiled his half smile, hit a switch, pulled a lever, and the shed filled with the engine's scream and the labored whine of metal chewing through wood. Each pass of the log removed a curved cant of bark and revealed the log's yellow interior. The smell of sap hung heavy in the cautious heat of early summer. I watched the pile of 2 x 6s and 1 x 10s grow with the glee of a child counting presents under a Christmas tree.

———

By June, my work with Gary was done. He loaned me a flatbed to haul my loot. I stacked and stickered the boards in the driveway of my rented cabin. Each morning on the way to my government job, I'd pause to admire that tarp-covered stack of lumber. Staring at that wood, I could believe I was damn near a homeowner. I could forget I had no money to buy land to assemble those boards into a house.

During my first summer as a biologist with the Park Service, I was given a skiff, camping gear, binoculars, and orders to go count birds or track bears. While exploring wild beaches or scrambling up mountain ridges, it was hard to believe I was actually being paid. I was certain the paychecks would stop when someone figured out how much fun I was having sleeping in moss-draped forests and brewing coffee over driftwood fires.

Turns out I was right; it was too good to be true. The checks kept coming, but the fun dried up like a puddle in a desert. In my second season, I counted fewer birds and pushed more papers. By my third year, I was plotting policies and muddling through management plans. Had I foreseen the tightening grip of the office I might have worked harder to keep my distance. Had I known my first position was the best job I'd ever have, I might have declined the promotions. But I needed the money, so I allowed myself to get reeled in.

While pay stubs collected in a deskside drawer, tension gathered in my back. While the boards in my driveway weathered to a dark brown, I sat behind a computer growing paler by the month. The calluses I'd grown with Gary had long since faded and peeled. My clothes were clean, free of tree pitch and beach mud. Soft fingers on a keyboard, stocking feet on an electronic foot warmer, I worked hard to pretend I was a biologist, not a bureaucrat.

Weekends I scrounged more stuff. I packed beams from the tide line, scavenged cracked doors from the dump. On a trip through Juneau I stopped by a glass company to ask what they had lying around. I was led to a long row of miscellaneous windows collecting dust in the back of the shop.

"These are ones customers never picked up. I'd be happy to move 'em," the clerk explained.

"How much?" I asked

"How 'bout ten bucks apiece?"

"Crate 'em," I said.

A month later the huge box was leaning against the boards in the driveway. I carefully pried open the crate and measured each window. Had Frank been alive, I would have sent the measurements his way, had him design the perfect home. I sent the numbers to Anya instead, along with a pad of graph paper. While my butt was conforming to the shape of an office chair, Anya's body was wedged in the confines of lecture hall seats. During boring seminars she scratched house designs and sent them my way. At my desk, in between staff meetings, I made little changes and shipped them back. Despite my efforts to let Anya go, we found ourselves, once again, drawn to the dream of a life neither one of us was living.

While Anya earned her degree, I earned enough money for a down payment. She graduated and returned to Gustavus with an MD after her name and four years of too little sleep and too much coffee in her body. She wisely took time off: a year free of lectures, exam rooms, and textbooks;

twelve months to pick berries, hike beaches, and sleep full nights before plunging into the rigors of residency.

We studied plat maps and rode our bikes all over town. We eventually found the perfect piece of ground: six acres of mixed forest and meadow cut by the pleasing curves of a little stream. We spent days on the land, imagining the garden in the sunny meadow, situating the root cellar in the forest shade. In our minds, we oriented the house just inside the trees, careful to keep the neighbors and road out of sight. The land, unfortunately, was more than I could ever afford. But, while napping with Anya beneath the purple blaze of lupine and lazy hum of bees, my affection for the place outgrew my aversion to debt.

While waiting for the bank and title company to shuffle and sign all the papers, we moved my jumble of boards, doors, and windows to the edge of the property. It was mid-July when the deed for the land showed up in the morning mail. That evening, bribed with cases of cold beer and the promise of hot spaghetti, a dozen friends helped haul the lumber across the meadow to the house site. Within twenty-four hours of owning land, I was digging a hole for the corner post of my home.

Evenings and weekends I bolted from the office, stripped off my clean khakis, and jumped into my pitch-stained jeans. Conferring with Anya's sketches and a library book on house framing, we pretended to be carpenters. Anya's wide imagination was constrained by my narrow skills. Since I could not imagine how to join the sixteen-foot boards together, the final house design was a two-story cube. We sawed wood, pounded nails, and scratched our heads through the construction of each wall.

Cranes passed directly overhead as I fit the last of Gary's boards onto the roof one evening in mid-September. My hammer fell silent as I gawked at each passing flock. After sinking the last nail, I climbed down the ladder, dropped my tool belt, and joined Anya in the skeleton of the house. A north breeze blew through the window openings and stirred the sawdust like drifting snow. As the September sun dropped toward the tree tops, another flock of cranes passed overhead. We leaned out the second story windows and twisted our heads skyward.

"Stay here," I told Anya. "I'll be right back." I jumped on my bike, pedaled to our rented cabin, and stuffed pads and sleeping bags into a pack. When I rolled back up the path, Anya was facing the setting sun, legs dangling from a second-story window. We swept the dust from the rough floorboards and unrolled our bags.

In a few weeks Anya would fly to Seattle for three years of residency. I would turn up the office foot warmer and settle in to digging my way out of debt. But when a few thousand more cranes dropped through the sunset into the wetlands west of our new home, none of that mattered. Filled with the sound of cranes, smell of sawdust, and satisfied ache of accomplishment, we sank onto our pads and zipped our bags against the evening chill. Steeped in what we'd done, we forgot for a while what we had yet to do.

The distant murmur of cranes grew with the deepening dark. The sound rose and fell like a stream burbling through a huge wooden pipe.

"It'll be too bad to put the glass in," Anya said. "It's nice to have the sounds blow through."

"Let's not. Let's call it done. Let's live just like this."

Chapter Seven

HOWLING WOLVES AND SLAMMING DOORS

EVERY ROAD IN GUSTAVUS IS A DEAD END. It takes a plane, a boat, or a hell-for-stout pair of hiking boots to actually leave town. I first drove the ten miles of dirt roads in a well-rusted yellow Datsun pickup that set me back $500.

"Mind the brakes," my neighbor said as he pocketed the check. "Rear right is the only one with any grip. Slam 'em hard and it'll jerk you right into the ditch."

I didn't really need brakes back then; the thick dust and deep ruts kept me, like most folks, from driving too fast. Stopping is easy when you're going slow. Like a drought discussed among farmers or salmon prices among fisherman, road conditions dominated our conversations.

"Getting bad, isn't it?"

"Hell yeah. Been pounding the piss out of my kidneys."

"Gets any worse I'm liable to bruise my brain."

We all recognized each other by the cars we drove. An arm out the window or a flash of the headlights meant stop and chat. It was a rare trip to the post office that I didn't encounter a pair of trucks parked in the middle of the road, elbows and hat brims poking through open windows, people jawboning about whatever. Unable to get around, I'd gladly coast to a stop and join the discussion. A half dozen or more people might gather. Beers emerged from the rubble of someone's truck. Dinner plans were made, political differences aired, fishing advice passed along, lost loves mourned.

"Well, gotta go."

"Yeah, me too. Got stuff to do."

Someone would start a truck and the meeting would end.

In just two generations the short stretch of Boston-born pavement, laid when my grandfather was a boy, arced across rivers and wound through mountain ranges, stretching from coast to coast. Even Gustavus, tucked into the folds of an Alaskan archipelago, could not escape. We were found out and the snake spread ten miles of smooth, quiet blackness before moving on.

I admit that I cursed the old road along with everyone else. I didn't like breathing the clouds of dust. I didn't like it when the bumper rattled off my truck, taking the headlights with it. But I also didn't like seeing the barge, heaped with gravel and trucks, pull into town. A batch plant was erected near the beach: a tall, foreign-smelling thing accentuated by a steady plume of smoke. All summer the batch plant dumped its belly-load of blackness into the mouths of stained trucks.

The kids were outfitted with new Rollerblades and skateboards in anticipation. They tried their new wheels on the still-steaming asphalt. They wobbled about, shrieked, and clung to each other for balance. That whole summer the steady whine of the paving machine woke me each morning and hung in my ears at night.

Changes to town were subtle yet irreversible. My old yellow truck lost its back bumper and then finally died altogether. It left town on a scrap metal barge jumbled high with other relics from the rough-road days, replaced now by shiny minivans, trucks with push-button windows, and sport cars with the clearance of sandbox toys.

As Yogi Berra said, "The future ain't what it used to be." Although we gained a smooth surface that didn't rattle our rigs and shake our kidneys, a lot got buried beneath the pavement. The saddest change for me was the loss of our middle-of-the-road meetings. The tradition lingered for a month or two. I made a point of waving people down whether I had anything to say or not. Folks stopped but rarely shut off the engines. Cars piled up but no one got out. People stayed in their rigs, tapping the wheel, afraid the snake would swallow idle cars. Conversations were rushed. Pretty soon they were not worth having at all.

———

We built our home several years before the pavement. During a lunch break, Anya and I rattled down the dusty road in the yellow Datsun to check the mail. On the way back to pound more nails, Sam's blue Ford, parked on the roadside, emerged from the dust like a ship in the fog. I coasted to a stop, careful not to touch the brakes. Sam was leaning against the driver's door, legs and arms folded, watching something across the road. Anya and I followed Sam's gaze to a black lump on the opposite shoulder. The lump lifted its head, looked our way, and then settled its muzzle back into the dust.

"Been there all night. First saw him before dark," Sam explained. "Was out walking the mutt. It was moving more then. Dragging itself along the ditch."

Sam is a gruff man with a heavily furred thick neck that slides in an easy curve into his massive chest and round belly. He owns a little poodle-type dog that he calls a "goddamn barking bedroom slipper." But when no one is looking, he slips the dog a treat from the pocket of his work shirt.

"What happened?" I asked

"All's I know is couple o' gunshots went off last night round supper time. Came from the direction of Tom's place. Weren't no rifle, sounded like a shotgun." The bear swung its head through the gravel.

"Why didn't you kill it last night?" I asked.

"No way. Out of season. State trooper have me filling out forms till my hand cramps up."

We leaned against Sam's truck a while, watching the dying bear. When we got back to the house site, I couldn't concentrate on carpentry.

"I think I'll get my gun," I told Anya, dropping my tool belt.

"I'll go with you."

When we returned, four cars were parked along the ditch, doors open, people quietly gathered around the hood of an old white pickup. Shelley, a nearby neighbor, told me the bear had dragged itself into the woods. I loaded my gun and stepped into the forest. Just beyond range of whispering voices, I glimpsed the bear. It lay between two pines, head up, looking at me. I braced the rifle against a tree. I centered the crosshairs below the round bumps of its ears. The gun roared. The head dropped. I slowly walked to the bear. The night-black fur rose and fell with slow breath. The hind legs, with a sudden kick, pushed the round body out from the tree. I raised the rifle to shoot again and then lowered it. The skull was already shattered. More bullets couldn't make it die any faster.

Anya was the first to reach me. I pulled her warmth under my arm. We stepped closer and saw a red, jellylike puddle pooled beside the slightly open mouth. The skin on the front shoulder and back leg trembled like a horse quivering to scare off flies. Anya and I have watched many deer die, have seen the shivering skin and the slow curling of legs. My father called it nerves. I see it as a draining of life, a slow slide that lingers after pulse and breath have stopped. I often leave deer after they are shot, take a walk to calm my pulse and return when the animal is still.

For some reason I did not leave the bear. I moved closer and sunk my fingers through the thick fur to the trembling skin. I was thankful for Anya's hand on my shoulder.

Shelley wound through the trees with a shovel. Anya and Shelley grabbed one front paw and I the other as we tugged the bear's bulk away from the pine to a forest opening.

"Digging will be easier here," Shelley said. "Not so many roots."

I sliced the shovel into the sandy soil. I was just starting to sweat when Tom arrived with another shovel and two knives. "I'll dig. Don't much like skinning," Tom said. Anya and I accepted the knives and began peeling hide from flesh. We were soon enveloped in the subtle waft of grease and musk.

Between heaves of the shovel, Tom told the story of noise on his porch. It was dark. He chased the bear down the stairs and fired a shotgun, aiming over the top of the fleeing animal. A bold bear. A bear self-taught in the lucrative but risky business of snitching human food. Tom did not mean to kill.

I have since chased many bears off my own porch. I use a slingshot instead of a shotgun. I send them down the path with a barrage of whizzing stones. I do my best to hit them hard. If I can get bears to associate houses with bruises instead of bread, perhaps they will not prowl for snacks at households that keep a loaded rifle inside the door.

Skinning Tom's bear, the soft thickness of fur gave way to the hard lines of marbled muscle. I couldn't help but think of the muscles wrapped around my own bones. I couldn't help but picture the resemblance of my own skinned form, peeled of personal identity and laid alongside the bear. When I found two places where pellets penetrated the hide and slid between ribs, lodging in the bear's belly, I thought of the slow burn, stomach juice and blood filling spaces where they shouldn't be.

"I wonder what the State will do with the hide? Sure would make a nice rug," Tom said, up to his waist in the bear's grave. Maybe Tom was trying to salvage something from the loss. Or maybe he was simply trying to penetrate the quiet that covered us like a cold fog. I slashed the hide in long parallel slices. There would be no rug.

———

Decades in front of the paving machines, pioneers pushed across the continent, shooting all the bears in their path. I am among the last of the pioneers. I can't go any farther west. Neither can the bears. Neither can the asphalt. So here we are, pinned between the encroaching urban world and the steady waves of the Pacific. The bears are being bears, pushed by a deep curiosity, drawn by a keen nose in the relentless search for calories. The people are being people, drawn to the quiet and charm of the wilds and comforts and convenience of modern living. The asphalt is being asphalt, covering the bumps, dips, and dust so the industrial revolution can roll smoothly on.

The bears did not invite the people, but the people invited the pavement. The paving was debated through a long series of town meetings. In the end there were no arguments more convincing than the old road itself, with its bone-jarring, truck-rattling ruts and choking clouds of dust. When the vote was finally tallied, my hand was one of the few raised in opposition. The town accepted the government's offer and we awaited our inclusion into the system of federal highways.

After the vote for government-sponsored pavement came the vote for government itself. When I first came to Gustavus, there was no mayor, no city council, no taxes, no cops. Technically we were not a city at all, just a group of folks living near one another. Neighbors pooled money to get the streets plowed. Someone organized a softball league. Someone else started up a landfill. Another group raised the funds for a library.

Overworked volunteers complained that the new arrivals did not understand the spirit of volunteerism. The same dedicated thirty people were doing the work for the whole community. Proponents of city government said we needed the teeth of law to get everyone to pay their share. They warned unregulated growth would scar the face of our pretty town. We needed planning money. We needed to get organized.

City opponents took the if-it-ain't-broke-don't-fix-it posture. They warned of government waste, the sour taste of regulations, overspent city budgets. The debate was lively and contentious. The vote happened in late winter. Turnout was high. We became a city by just a few votes.

Not only did I check "yes," but I put my name on the ballot. I agreed local government was a tool needed to shape the town's inevitable growth. I took a seat on the first city council for the same reasons I served on the board of two conservation groups, for the same reason I wrote letters to editors, governors, and senators. Without organized resistance, the insanity that passed for progress would never stop.

I explained to the new city council that every metropolis on the continent was, at some point, the size of our dear town. Bears once sniffed along the Atlantic coast for food. The only difference between Galveston and Gustavus was time. The pattern is clear but we can do it differently, I said. We can preserve quiet evenings and dark nights, promote gratitude instead of growth. I suggested a carbon tax and a communal bike repair shop. I supported sliding fees for our community clinic. I'd ask at the beginning of a meeting if anyone else had heard the wolves howling last night. No one had.

Tolerance for my ideas quickly thinned to impatience and then lightly veiled hostility. Perpetual progress, I soon realized, was the underlying gospel, an assumed mission and starting point for the council. I was the token heretic, the lone pain-in-the-ass and impediment to the work at hand. New city letterhead and crisp business cards were cheap tickets into the offices of senators and congresspeople. The trough of public money runs deep and my fellow councilmen couldn't scarf it up fast enough. Soon we were lined up for a new dock, new runway lights, new boat harbor, new graveyard, new landfill. The plow of ambition that cut across the prairie was cutting through my hometown.

After a particularly discouraging council meeting, I took a walk to the wide wetlands west of town. My friend Shar Fox joined me. She was in town for a few days, getting a break from the bustle of cars and buses passing her downtown Juneau home. We were just past the end of the road when the first wolf howled. Shar and I stopped midstep and tilted our ears toward the rich call. We cocked our heads off to the right when the second wolf answered. Then the whole pack joined in, calling from all sides. The animals were close, moving through the sparse trees across the open wetlands. The howls drifted toward each other and then erupted into a cacophony of yips and barks as the pack reunited.

When the animals fell silent, Shar turned to me, eyes moist with gratitude. A whispered "wow" was all she could manage. We stood for a while to see if the wolves would start back up. A few mosquitoes buzzed in the wide silence. We slowly started for home, boots sloshing loudly through the wetlands.

Shar floated along, moving through the echoes. I tromped beside her, braced against a future of slamming doors. Where Shar saw willows and pines aglow in evening light, I saw the plat map that had the open country around us neatly divided into one-acre house lots. Gripped by a fear of the future, my mind magnified each small change: each new home would spread the seeds of sprawl; each new car would edge us another step closer to congestion and stoplights. The looming losses drained the beauty from my day.

What I didn't share with Shar, what I hadn't told the city council, what I couldn't even admit to myself was my frustration in feeling my own feet in lock-step with progress marching over beauty. Bears used to snuffle for berries where my house stands. The boards for my home came from a mile-long canyon I cut through a forest to push a dead-end road a little farther west. Having moved to Gustavus to get away from the urbanization of America, I couldn't accept that part of me was glad the asphalt had come, glad that I could ride my bike without plugging my lungs with dust. Not knowing how to yell at myself, I got mad at everyone else.

Shar and I paused before stepping onto the road leading back to town. A ruby-crowned kinglet fluttered from a willow tree behind us and snapped an insect from the air. The evening was so still that we could hear the quick snip, snip, snip of that tiny beak.

"Bring your grandkids here," I told Shar, "and the wolves will be gone. Stand right here and the sound of bird beaks will be buried beneath pounding hammers and whining lawnmowers." I continued my rant as we walked the road back to the house. I dragged my friend into the future of leaf blowers and barking dogs, motorbikes and screaming kids. Shar didn't try to stop me. She listened with silent patience. But before we climbed the steps into the house she turned me with a touch on the arm. She placed a hand on my chest and said,

"Hank, the wolves are still here."

Chapter Eight

A BEAR, A BEAVER, AND BOB

I STOOD NAKED ON THE BOW, gave a whoop, and dove in. The cold clamped down like a giant fist. I stroked hard back to the boat, hauled myself over the gunwale, and sat panting and dripping next to Anya. "Nutball," she said.

"It feels so good as soon as you're out."

Our boat floated in the center of Icy Strait, halfway between Gustavus and Lemesurier Island. No wind; a rarity for this exposed stretch of water. The fetch to the north was a full seventy miles to where icebergs jostled in the turbid waters of Glacier Bay. No land for fifty miles to buffer the dominant southeast winds. The familiar hills of Lemesurier beckoned eight miles to the west. The dark line of the Gustavus Flats stretched away to the east.

It was June, peak summer. The sea roiled with the month's biggest tide, tugging and twisting the boat. The deep green water was thick with life: specks of plankton, waving arms of jellycombs, jittering amphipods, and tight schools of glittering fish. Clumps of seaweed spun in the sinuous tiderip. The peeping whistle of murrelets came from all directions and dozens of the small seabirds paddled about with silver needlefish pinched in their bills. Thousands of kittiwake gulls circled the rips like feathered confetti. When a ball of fish neared the surface, the gulls swarmed in a screaming feeding frenzy. The wide-eyed face of a harbor seal watched our boat from a wary distance.

"Must be hell being a bait fish," Anya said.

"Yeah," I agreed, pulling a shirt over goose-bumped skin. "Spend all day trying to get away from bird beaks and fish teeth and then a whale swallows you and everyone you've ever known." I turned the key and the outboard's rumble buried the sounds of Icy Strait. The boat skimmed across the flat water as I eased the throttle forward. Murrelets, cormorants, and guillemots dove to escape the speeding hull. I steered wide curves around the misty breath of whales rising and falling across the strait.

I'd navigated to the island countless times since moving to Gustavus. In the course of those visits, I had gotten to know John Kibbons, the current owner of an old homestead nestled into a cove along the island's southern shore. Most winters John traded the solitude of the island for a warm beach in Baja. He encouraged me to check in on the place while he was away. I was glad to oblige and made the trip across Icy Strait as frequently as weather and work allowed.

When Anya was in school or doctoring in Juneau, I snuck off to the island to hunt and be alone, to escape newscasts and papers, to forget all that was wrong with the world. Unlike Gustavus, no one was trying to improve the place; there were no government plans to stimulate the island's economy, no list of capital improvement projects. The same cold currents and high winds that made it hard for me to get to the island meant the snake of asphalt was unlikely to slither onto her shores. In recent years, John had found another caretaker, Bob Christensen, willing to be on the island full time. Fortunately, Bob was happy to share his adopted island home with me.

I was still chilled from my swim as we nosed up the creek. Bob splashed through thigh-deep water using a long pole to herd a half dozen drift logs up the tide-swollen stream. I jumped ashore and he tossed me a line. "Good timing," Bob said, prodding his prizes closer to the beach. "That's as far as they're going. Snug 'em up and tie 'em off." Bob waded ashore to give me a hug.

"You guys bring something for lunch?" he asked. "I'm starving."

"I got you covered, Bobby," Anya said, coming in for a squeeze.

We hauled our cartload of groceries and gear across the wide skirt of lawn to the old red-roofed house. Foxglove flowers stood brilliant against the gray shingle siding. Rosebuds grew thick on a wide tangle of thorns. I never got to meet Joe and Muz Ibach, the couple that built the house and planted flowers in the yard. After nearly forty years of solitary island living, they had died just a few years before I was born.

I studied the Ibachs' photo on the living room wall while Anya unloaded sandwich fixings on the kitchen counter. In faded black and white, Joe and Muz Ibach stand together in the doorway we just came through. Joe is looking at the camera, Muz looking at Joe. Age has grayed both their heads. Joe's thin frame is bent by the years, while Muz stands thick and straight. Muz has a hand tucked into the crook of Joe's elbow. She looks proud in a starched white shirt. Joe seems relaxed, wearing hip boots like he just came in for lunch after some chore in the creek. Both are smiling with a sweetness that makes you wish they could be your grandparents.

Sandwiches ready, we sat at the table overlooking the yard, Muz's rosebush, and the small marker at the head of the couple's grave. "How long can you stay?" Bob asked, mouth full of smoked salmon.

"A few days; enough time to get those logs cut and split and kick your butt in horseshoes."

"You could be here a long time before you beat me at shoes."

"Longer the better."

———

Lemesurier Island is an up and down place. The terrain rises and dips like a huge wad of paper crumpled by giant hands. It takes two days to hike around the perimeter. It takes a couple lifetimes to explore the interior gullies and ridges. From a distance the island appears draped by feathered green fur. On foot the towering forest is broken by muskegs, hidden ponds, sheer cliffs, and wind-blown hillsides.

Half the island is limestone formed four hundred million years ago somewhere south of the equator. The slow northward twist of the Pacific Ocean's floor smeared the rock onto Alaska's coast. The magmatic activity from the collision of the two plates produced an intrusion of granite that forms the other half of the island. The contact is straddled by a skinny mile-long lake. The lake's inlet stream flows over granite cobbles. The outlet is a limestone sinkhole jammed with logs and sticks. Water drains down the sinkhole with a deep sucking sound and never resurfaces.

The island's high point is a two thousand five hundred-foot domed summit sculpted by the Wisconsin Ice Sheet. Up close the rock is eroded into knife-edge veins that drop into fluted, twisting caverns. In between clusters of wind-battered spruce and mountain hemlock lies a delicate carpet of mountain heathers, copper bush, purple-mountain and leather-leafed saxifrages, spleen warts, and maiden hair fern.

On the lower slopes the trees stretch for the light, still gray columns rising from a continuous bed of moss. An abundance of deer keep the understory nibbled down to stubs and leave the forest floor spacious and wide. In contrast to the steady presence of deer, the island's human history is sporadic and sparse. The Tlingit call the island *Taas' Daa* (Double-headed Tide Island) in reference to the twin dome summits arcing above tree line. Squat in the center of Icy Strait, the island cleaves the tidal currents connecting the convoluted Inside Passage with the open ocean. During times of warfare, the Tlingit occupied a fort site atop limestone cliffs along the eastern shore of Taas' Daa. The perch afforded a panoramic view to scan for unfamiliar canoes. Rock art—spirals and circles perhaps carved by apprehensive warriors—is still visible on the cliff face.

In 1794, George Vancouver sailed a fleet of three boats past the island while probing for the elusive Northwest Passage. The captain of HMS *Chatham* named the island after his midshipman William Le Mesurier. Like a stray mutt lifting his leg in some other dog's territory, the cartographer scratched the homesick sailor's name on the chart, ignoring centuries of local human history. Had there been a salmon run, consistent berry crop, or some other cornerstone of subsistence economy, Vancouver may have seen smoke from a permanent Tlingit settlement. Instead, the island's first year-round residents showed up a hundred and fifty years after Vancouver's three ships sailed by.

Joe Ibach was just shy of twenty when he left his native New York. Sick of the clamor and commerce of cities, he headed for the distant wilds of Alaska. He worked his way across the continent to Seattle, where he wrangled passage on a steamer to Prince William Sound. Partnering with other young pioneers, he quickly learned the lucrative trade of farming foxes. In 1908, he met and married Muz in the town of Cordova. There is no record of why or how the young couple traveled across the Gulf of Alaska to the rainforest of Southeast. We do know that after rowing their boat up the creek at Lemesurier in 1920, they never moved again. With a broad axe and bow saw, Joe cobbled together a twelve-by-twelve-foot log house, the first of many structures he built on the island. With a roll of chicken wire and bundle of 2 x 2s, Joe nailed together long, low-slung pens to confine the foxes whose furs provided the couple's cash. With loads of kelp Muz transformed river gravel into a fertile garden. Old photos show the front yard festooned with thigh-high potato plants and shoulder-high foxglove flowers.

In 1921 the U.S. Department of Agriculture made Taas' Daa, owned by the Takdeintaan clan, part of the Tongass National Forest. Surveyors drew the forest boundary around the Ibachs' place, leaving them five acres of private land surrounded by public forest. That plot of ground served as their home base for the next four decades. When Muz fell ill in 1959, Joe got her to the hospital seventy miles away in Juneau. If Joe had known Muz would not return, he might have stayed on the island, letting her die within view of the garden she loved. Left alone, Joe didn't last a year. Before he shot himself, he scratched a simple note: "There is a time to live and a time to die. Now is the time."

———

A few years after Bob settled on the island, a lone bear showed up. We don't know where the bear dens, but each spring he emerges to nip the new ryegrass shoots poking up along the shore. Lemesurier is a hungry place for a bear; there are no salmon streams, sedge flats, or berry patches. All summer he prowls the island's perimeter, snuffling up sand fleas, rooting up ground cone, and gobbling the occasional tide-tossed fish. It's a tough life; he's a scrawny bear. I don't know why he stays.

The beaver lived alone in a jumble of sticks on the shore of the lake. He might have dammed up the outflow stream if it wasn't swirling down the sinkhole. The beaver swam laps in the deep cold lake, slapping the surface with his tail, hoping to attract a mate that never came. Eventually, he either left or died; we'll never know.

We can only guess at what inspired the beaver and the bear to step into the frigid sea and swim off for an uncertain life on the island. Bob left Bellingham in search of a place to quiet his brain's incessant internal chatter. He launched a self-built kayak and, ninety-six days of solo paddling later, found himself floating off the island's southern shore, gawking at the red-roofed house on the apron of lawn.

As Bob studied the homestead with binoculars he noticed a man in the yard, staring back through his own binoculars. Bob quickly grabbed the pole off his deck and pretended to fish. When his pole bent in half and a giant halibut started dragging his kayak around the cove, he forgot about the house. Seeing his predicament, the man on the beach rowed out, helped land the fish, and invited Bob in for a visit.

Over a meal of steamed halibut and garden greens, John shared the homestead's history. He laid out photos and told stories of the Ibachs' early years and Joe's love-torn decision to take his life. Bob helped with the dishes as John explained that Joe and Muz had willed the place to the mail-boat captain who checked in with the Ibachs in their later years. John was living in Juneau when the captain put the place up for sale and John snatched it up. Over brandy, John mentioned he was looking for a live-in winter caretaker.

Fifteen years after landing that halibut, Bob was still spending winters on the island, mostly in solitude. The first winter, without anyone to talk to, Bob filled his time by trying not to talk to himself. Day after day, month after month, he went into the forest, stood in one spot, and waited for his brain to shut up. The moments slowly came, fleeting and elusive, but blissfully free of language; no voices of doubt or judgment, no monologues about a troubling past or worrisome future. The second winter, the quiet moments stretched wider and wider. The vacuum of words filled with what Bob describes as a subtle vibrancy flickering through the still forest. A faint shift in light, the touch of wind on his cheek consumed his awareness.

"Turns out words don't really work to describe wordless experiences," Bob said.

"How long do the moments last?"

"Not sure. Takes words to tell time."

Bob's been toying with altered states since boyhood. Fresh out of high school, he decided to fast for thirty days, consuming nothing but water—a regimen that would kill most people.

"I tried fasting once," I said.

"How'd it go?" asked Bob.

"Started out good, but around midday I got hungry so I ate lunch."

Bob remembers his fast as one of the finer moments in life. At the time, he lived in a condemned house in a rough Spokane neighborhood. Unable to afford bus fare, he walked the ten miles to attend painting classes at a community college. "I was doing great, it was my ego that starved and shriveled. I just remember the leaves and birdsong becoming increasingly brilliant each day." In addition to art, Bob was enrolled in a barbecuing class. Around day fifteen of the fast, while preparing a fruit salad to complement the day's pork chops, he was tempted by a slice of fresh strawberry.

"I'd have eaten that thing," I said. "That is the difference between you and me."

"One of many, Hankster."

Bob's calm remains even in the face of pain. One winter, stormed-in alone on the island, his cheek swelled with pressure from an abscessed tooth. Deep in the night with the infection climbing toward his brain, he went into the tool room to experiment with dentistry. He worked through an array of pliers, but they all slipped off the tooth. Using the pointed end of a steel file, he finally managed to pry the throbbing molar loose.

"Did you say a bad word when you did that?" I asked.

"Couldn't. Had a file in my mouth."

"Did you scream?"

"Nope. It took all my concentration to stay conscious."

———

The tide dropped during lunch, stranding the logs on the creek gravels. Bob sharpened the chainsaw while I gathered up the splitting tools. I rolled each round above the tideline after Bob cut it free with the snarling saw. With the first log bucked, Bob shut off the saw and picked up the sledgehammer. Driving the steel wedge, he cracked each wide round in half. I followed behind, breaking the chunks into stove-size pieces with the maul. With each blow, saltwater sprayed from the wood.

"It'll take a couple years for this to dry," I said.

"No worries. We'll be here when it's ready," Bob replied.

At first, I found Bob a frustrating addition to the island, his perpetual calm an irritation. I'd try to ruffle him up by sharing passages from books about peak oil or religious fanaticism. Bob would listen patiently then ask, "Why do you read that crap? It just gets you all riled up."

"The world is getting trammeled, Bob. Don't you care?"

"Sure I do. But I also believe worry is like praying for what you don't want."

When Bob planted a satellite dish alongside the rosebush and brought the World Wide Web to the Ibachs' place, I bristled at the intrusion.

"It's like pavement in the wilderness," I told him. "It just doesn't belong." Bob beamed back his calm look.

"A computer is an inert machine, Hank. It can't hurt you. It's the effort of escape that forms the chains of your imprisonment."

Whatever, I thought, *no use arguing with a monk.*

Turns out, however, monks are often right; beware debating anyone who has months of solitude to ponder their position. After many rainy forest walks and long evening talks, it became clear that Bob and I came to the island for different reasons. Bob was captivated by what was here; I was drawn to what wasn't. Bob came looking forward; I showed up looking over my shoulder. Bob knew my dismay with progress traveled to the island with me as surely as the gear in my boat. The boat is easy to unload. I didn't know where to begin to clean out my head.

Through the years, my affection for the island and Bob has deepened. I now want to get to the island more than I want to leave town. Bob is again right; it is easier to see where you are when you're not looking over your shoulder.

I want to be buried on the island. Not beneath the mowed grass alongside Joe and Muz, but in a little pocket of muskeg on the far side of the lake. I go to the spot each year while I am hunting. I imagine the plants growing over my grave, the deer walking over my jumble of bones.

Last fall I took Bob to the spot so he would know. It took us a couple hours of hiking to get there. Bob asked if it would be all right if he strapped a steel cone to my head and dropped me from a helicopter. He figures a free fall from five hundred feet ought to auger me in all the way to my ankles. When I hesitated, Bob sweetened the deal by offering to hike up later and place a nice bouquet between my feet.

Chapter Nine

SNAPSHOT

AFTERNOONS WERE HARDEST. Stomach heavy with lunch, my eyelids drooped and my mind wandered from the screen before me to the memories alive somewhere beyond the office walls. I often fantasized of heaving a file cabinet's worth of management plans into the dumpster, waving a casual farewell to my office mates, and stepping from the workplace sterility into the thrumming pulse of the real world. Instead, I ambled over to the coffee machine, poured another cup, and tried not to look at the clock ticking ever so slowly toward the end of the day.

It is ironic that my office, situated in the midst of the largest swath of public lands on the planet, felt closer to the pace of politics in far-off D.C. than to the musing of a monk on a nearby island. The millions of jumbled acres of Glacier Bay National Park bordered the unfathomably larger eleven-million-acre expanse of Wrangell-St. Elias National Park. Given enough stamina and food, a person could scramble and climb for weeks on end over mountain ranges, ice fields, and watersheds the size of Texas without encountering so much as a cigarette butt. Anyone was free to spend a lifetime poking around the seventeen million acres of estuaries, valleys, and islands comprising the Tongass National Forest. It's odd that America, home of the free market, proponent of private ownership, birthplace of the Big Mac, is also running the largest experiment in communal land ownership in the world.

The experiment, viewed from my desk, was not going well. I'd pull into work each morning, flip on the computer, and wade through a stream of reports from the war between preservation and profit, conservation and capitalism. I was not surprised when *Consumer Reports* ran an article (sandwiched between an assessment of SUVs and a shopper's guide to toothpaste) comparing the country's national parks. Turned out Glacier Bay was ranked number one, the best buy for the traveling tourist. Natural beauty is a hot commodity and Glacier Bay was a gold mine of scenery and bears, puffins and whales.

I believed in the mission of the park service. I wanted to do my part to say the planet is not a product, beauty cannot be bought, and mystery is not mere merchandise. I'd worked my way to the table of "decision makers" managing a place I loved. But I had little faith in the dispassionate language of policies and plans. Government writing is stiff and distant. No personal pronouns. No expressions of love. How can a real dialogue about the human relationship to the landscape flow from such a dry place?

I was committed to conservation but bored with bureaucracy. I was grateful for my job but convinced there was more fulfilling work to be done. I dreamed of living close to the land but found myself eating prepackaged pocket pizzas for lunch. But I did not yet own the ground under my house. My mortgage was bigger than my desires.

The bulk of each paycheck got sent off to the bank. It took eight years to whittle that mountain of debt down to a little mound. Still, it was not an easy decision to quit. My supervisor offered paid training, another promotion. At a conference of wilderness managers, I was given the Howling Wolf Award for the person most likely to make a difference. I could see what I was going to be when I grew up. My retirement account was growing. Paid vacation accrued with each pay stub.

"You have to stay," co-workers counseled. "The Park needs you."

Maybe they were right. Maybe I wouldn't be able to make a difference from the "outside." Maybe it was irresponsible to quit. It was Ed, with his big belly and sore back, who helped clarify my decision. The enthusiasm marking the beginning of his career had long ago been displaced by cynicism. He pulled me aside one afternoon in midwinter and offered the following warning: *Be careful what you get good at; you'll spend the rest of your life doing it.*

I gave notice the following day and a month later walked out the office door for the last time. With my final paycheck, I made my last land payment. I was thirty years old, had $75 in the bank, and had never felt more free.

———

Two days after quitting, my alumni association happened to call.

"Mr. Lentfer, this is Ann at Evergreen State College," said the tentative young voice. "I'm calling to update our records. Are you still employed as a biologist?"

"No, I'm happily unemployed."

"Um . . . well . . . will you be finding another line of work soon?"

"Not if I can avoid it."

Ann chuckled nervously. I let the awkward silence hang for a moment before asking, "You haven't got a little box on your form for the intentionally unemployed, have you?"

"No."

"You are going to forget this conversation ever happened, aren't you?"

"I think that would be easiest."

A few weeks after cleaning out my desk, I traveled south to help Anya clean out her apartment. After three years confined by the corridors of a hospital, Anya was done. I'd like to say it was a joyous reunion, but our lives had drifted too far. Through the first year of residency, we had written long letters and run up a huge phone bill. Anya had flown to

Gustavus whenever she could scrap a few days free from training, arriving exhausted and pale. In trying to squeeze a season of living into those fleeting visits, we succeeded only in filling our time together with too much frustration, not enough fun.

During Anya's second year, intimacy could no longer span the distance. The letters shortened and the phone calls became less frequent. I invited other women into the widening space between us. In between day-long stints in the clinic and all-night watch in the delivery room, Anya had little time to worry about who was sharing meals with me in our little cabin.

By the third year, our relationship had shrunk to a distant hope. I boarded the plane to Seattle unsure whether I was opening my arms to a new life together or closing the door on an old dream. Anya knew only that she was tired and needed to find the place where the physician ended and the woman began. She needed to trade beeper and stethoscope for berry bucket and knitting needles, needed to move from under the fluorescent flicker into the shimmering rain.

Anya had a year off before putting her doctoring skills to work. Unsure about being together but unwilling to split apart, we returned to Gustavus. The garden was choked with weeds, the woodshed only half full, the few venison steaks and fish fillets in the freezer crowded by frozen burritos. As I pulled weeds and killed slugs in the garden, I watched the top of Anya's bent back as she plied the grassy meadow in search of strawberries like a contented bear.

Freed from lecture halls and staff meetings, Anya and I traveled through the calendar of berries, our days swayed by wind and tide. The strawberries near the garden are the first to ripen. Blueberries swell into late July and hold their color through the end of August. Nagoonberries peak mid to late August. Red huckleberries are best from late August through the first weeks of September. We boated from young river deltas to old forests, camping near the best patches, falling asleep to the song of hermit thrushes, waking to the tapping of rain. We cooked fresh fish over smoky fires, breaking the greasy flakes of flesh with our fingers. We bathed in frigid streams and drank tea on beaches alive with birds and bears. While searching for those berries, we found what we needed most: day after uninterrupted day to weave our worlds back together, to breathe and walk through the same place, to sleep and dream side by side.

On a sunny afternoon, boating home with buckets of berries and a tote of sockeye salmon, we fell in line with a pod of orcas. From dolphin-sized babies to thirty-foot males, the whales cruised along both sides of the skiff. We could see their black-and-white shapes passing under water, the surface boiling with each powerful thrust of their wide tails. I tried to imagine how many thousands of silvery salmon it took to nourish those sleek creatures. The iced fish in our cooler, enough to feed Anya and me for the year, the larger whales could eat in a single afternoon. The whales broke the surface again and again with explosive blows of breath. Occasionally a whale leapt from the water, arcing gracefully between green depths and bright sun.

Back in Gustavus we chased the persistent weeds and slimy slugs out of the garden once again. I split wood and stuffed the shed full. Anya processed berries into jelly and jam. I built a smokehouse and then cured a batch of fillets. Anya helped me finish the root cellar, spending hours on the back end of a shovel. "This is so much easier then doctoring," Anya said, pausing to straighten her aching back. "There is no way to do it wrong."

Come August, we made our way to Frank's Mountain. It had been three years since Anya last made the climb. Richard, as always, showed up. My dad came too, along with Anya's mom. The five of us sorted gear and loaded our packs on the beach under a high gray sky. By midafternoon we were entering the forest and starting the slow climb through a tangle of head-high devil's club and blueberry bushes. After two hours of steady stepping and sweating, we emerged from forest shade to the open air of a subalpine muskeg. We glimpsed the mountaintop a few miles away, streaked with patches of late-summer snow.

We walked for another hour along trails worn to bare dirt by generations of deer. When we reached the familiar campsite on the mountain's shoulder, we dropped our loads and stretched our tired backs. We strung tarps to shed the threatening rain. As the evening slid into the rich hues of twilight, we huddled together over mugs of cocoa. Pink-tinged peaks rose from the black forest and the deep indigo of straits and coves.

We awoke at dawn to dense fog. Anya and Richard slipped into the mist to the west. Dad and I went east and sat on the lip of a vast cloud-filled bowl. Judy had the sense to stay in bed. Sitting shoulder to shoulder, my father and I peered into the thick gray, straining to glimpse the deer we could hear nipping and chewing just below us. After long minutes, a whiff of wind stirred the clouds. The deer shifted into view. The echo of Dad's rifle rumbled back across the valley.

While we gutted and skinned, the crack of Richard's rifle carried from the other side of the mountain. We met back at camp as the wind gathered strength and blew the morning into brilliant blue. We sprawled out on the mountain heather, napping before the long descent to the beach. I was just about asleep, the hum of the mountain in my ears, the sweet weight of Anya's head on my chest when she asked me what I was thinking.

"Umm . . . nothing. And you?"

"Just thinking about baby names."

"Whose baby?" I asked

"Umm . . . I dunno."

————

High-bush cranberries grow within walking distance of the house. We harvested the tart fruit in the blustery days of late September. Clouds the size of countries sailed overhead, leaving shifting holes of blue.

Cranes scuttled and called, sifting south with the wind. We worked the edge of the wetlands, icy fingers pulling clumps of salmon-egg-red berries off the head-high bushes and dropping them into buckets strung from our necks. After days of picking, we had thirty gallons of berries stashed on the porch. We juiced the berries and filled sixty quart jars with the thick, bloodlike pulp. Thinned with water and sweetened with sugar, each jar yields a gallon of juice and the nostalgic taste of fall.

An early October frost slapped the garden and wilted all but the kale. We dug the spuds first. Each hill revealed a dozen or more tightly packed, fist-sized potatoes. As we dug into the carrots, I heard a raven call and looked up to see our neighbor, Kim Heacox, strolling up the path. His pitch-perfect bird imitation fools me every time. I often think I hear him announcing his arrival only to see a raven fly overhead.

Kim is a fellow Park Service dropout. He gave up the steady paycheck for the uncertain life of a writer and photographer. When invited to career day at the local high school, Kim showed up in his bathrobe. "This is my uniform," he told the kids. "My work day starts whenever I wake up. Sometimes that doesn't happen until lunch."

Bending over a carrot row, pulling up the last of the orange stalks, Kim started singing Steve Winwood's "Can't Find My Way Home." I joined in the melody and Kim slipped into high harmonies. It was a crisp, squally day; wind-tossed sunlight sprayed across the meadow. When a small flock of late-fall cranes billowed past, we quit singing and straightened up to watch. The low sun burned a rich gold as we washed the last of the carrots, numb fingers aching in the cold water.

"I've got to get a picture of this," said Kim, admiring our harvest.

"Do we have time?" I asked, eyeing the sun just above tree line to the west.

"Empty the root cellar! I'll run for the camera."

While Kim sprinted home, Anya and I hauled hundreds of jars from the root cellar out to the meadow. We hastily stacked the jars on the rungs of a stepladder and on boards propped on buckets. We piled up the spuds alongside the wheelbarrow full of glistening carrots. Kim returned, panting, and burned several frames as the pointed shadows of trees crept across the garden.

The photo is thumbtacked to our wall, a snapshot of a living dream. The light is gold. Anya and I stand arm in arm in the middle of jars of red juice, brown salsa, blue and maroon jam, and red fish. We look at each other with pleasure as deep as the fall glow. I see memories of Uramuro in that photo. I see Greg's example and Frank's satisfaction. I see the contentment of all three men, gratitude born in staying put. I see the friendship and music of neighbors. But mostly I see two people drawn together by their love for the same piece of earth.

Chapter Ten

SNOW

THE TWENTY THOUSAND SANDHILLS migrating through Gustavus and on up the Pacific Coast is a sidestream compared to the great river of birds flowing through the continent's interior. The first flocks drop into Nebraska's Platte River in late February. Through March, thousands more drift in from wintering grounds along the western Gulf Coast through Texas, southern New Mexico, Arizona, and northern Mexico. A half million cranes, the world's largest concentration, gather along an eighty-mile stretch of river known as the Big Bend Reach: a braided, shallow slip of water surrounded by agricultural fields. They feast on waste corn, find new mates, or renew affinities with old ones.

Mated pairs often separate in the winter, yet in their cacophony on the Platte they somehow find each other. When they do, they dance, flinging sticks and grass stems with their bills, bowing, leaping, legs akimbo, wing feathers spread wide. Then, standing side by side, bills tilted to the sky, they sing a duet, the unison call: two or three notes from the female answered quickly by the male—two birds, one sound echoing back through a million springs.

At night the birds roost wing to wing, crowded into the shallow waters and gravel islands of the river. At daybreak they billow and resettle into the adjacent fields to feed on corn left behind by the combines. Never are they quiet. In the dark, the landscape purrs with their collective chatter, as if the quiet river suddenly found its voice. In the growing light the cranes ruffle their feathers, stretch a wing to the side, a leg straight back, restless to feed, to fly.

The flock yearns north. The memory of migration ripples in growing murmurs as spring approaches. Birds can sense barometric pressure, a weather station tucked into the folds of each tiny brain. Sometime in early April, when the forecast is right, the carpet of birds lifts from the prairie and spills toward the Arctic.

Cranes are visual migrants; they match rivers and ridges to unique mental maps. They cover up to five hundred miles a day, winging from wetland to wetland. At each stop, they dance, pairs rising and falling through dusk and dawn, creating waves in a sea of gray bodies. Farther north, the threads of birds scatter across the landscape, some drifting toward Quebec, others toward Alaska's tundra, still others across the Bering Sea to Siberia. The strands break smaller and smaller as cranes fan across the Arctic until, finally, single pairs set their wings and drop through the chilly polar air to the same tundra pond or river delta they left eight months before.

When they arrive, they once again dance. And they sing: three notes and the answering fourth, over and over, with no one to hear, save maybe an Arctic fox or a loon.

——

My own courtship dance lasted well over a decade, choreographed by twin tensions of affection and fear. I was simultaneously drawn to Anya's bright smile and held back by my own desire for independence. Our common love of place seemed too precious to last, Anya's devotion more than I deserved.

The turning point in my courtship was a gift from a man who never intended to give it. Jon Traibush lived a few miles north of my place.

Whenever we met we headed for the nearest cribbage board. The bet was always the same: five bucks for the game, a dollar a corner, and ten cents a point. All bets doubled with a skunk, quadrupled with a double skunk. Jon shuffled with quick flips of the wrist and dealt the cards with flawless efficiency. "C'mon, c'mon. This is a fast-moving game," he would chide me whenever I took too long pondering my hand. He played the game the same way he lived, flitting from one project to the next with the enthusiasm of an overstimulated first-grader. "Hurry up! You can't win if you don't play."

Jon had lived in Gustavus for twenty-three years. He was a social pinball, bouncing from post office to hardware store to dock to dinner to poker game. "There are only two kinds of people in the world," Jon once told me. "You got your assholes and you got your dipwads."

"And what kind of person are you?" I asked, shuffling the cards.

"Oh, that's easy. I'm a definite dipwad."

"And me?"

"No-brainer. You're an asshole."

When pressed for definitions, Jon changed the subject. This was the beauty of his philosophy: by lumping the entire human species into two equally demeaning categories, he ignored social cliques and notions of class. He didn't care what social circle he entered—just don't ask him to stay very long.

The first flakes of the year had slipped past my window in the prolonged dusk of mid-November. I finished my tea and shrugged into the weight of winter clothes. The path to Jon's house wound through a spruce forest crowding the banks of a quiet river. A mile from home I could hear the thuds of Jon's hammer. He was framing the second story of his boat shed, a huge building that grew beneath his perpetually working body. Most people pack up their tools in winter. Jon simply layered on another coat and kept on building. When I walked up the driveway, he finished a cut and set down the saw.

"Hey, neighbor. Coffee? Time for a game?"

We stomped our feet on the porch and brushed the snow off our arms before settling in by the cribbage board, where we sank into the rhythm of dealing, shuffling, and pegging points. The conversation drifted from predicted snow to who's in Mexico, who's splitting up, whose car was parked in whose driveway early in the morning last week. Jon cheered the new romances, a reflection of the happiness that had been filling his days for several years, ever since Mary Cook stepped into his life. Jon had a build-it-and-she-will-come philosophy of carpentry and romance. It worked. At a party one night, Jon asked the new girl in town if she was interested in breakfast. He went home alone, but Mary knocked on his door early in morning, came in for coffee, and never left.

We played three games before Jon went back to his carpentry. I lost two, one by a skunk, and left owing Jonny $31.

The next day, winter stuttered and turned the snow into sleet and then rain. I hunched to see through the low half-circle of glass cleared by the laboring defroster in my old truck. Through the half-open side window, I glimpsed an arm waving from my neighbor's orange pickup. I followed Lewis into the horseshoe driveway of the gas station. Engines still running, windows rolled down, Lewis asked, "Where have you been? Have you heard?"

"I've been out for an hour or so—bailing my boat. Heard what?" Lewis looked down, silent long enough for me to know that the news was not good.

"Jonny is dead. Fell off the roof of his boat shed. Sometime this afternoon. That's all I know."

When I got back to the house, the phone was ringing. A rumble was moving through town. People called each other not only to spread the news but to seek help in trying to accept it, as if more people knowing would somehow make Jon less gone.

My house grew small. I paced for a while and then left. Without knowing why or what I expected to find, I swung the truck down the rutted slick road to Jon and Mary's house. Mary was on the couch, curled in a blanket. She looked impossibly small, as though an invisible arm had punched her in the stomach. Before that moment, I'd seen Mary as Jonny's new girlfriend. But death invites intimacy. I slipped behind Mary on the couch and held her shrunken body to my chest.

The rest of the day was a bizarre blur. Neighbors came and went, delivering one casserole after another. Two of the local Mormons showed up in suits and ties and stood awkwardly in the corner until God or something dismissed them from their duty. A case of Rainier beer appeared on the coffee table and people sucked it down, working hard to keep pace with the tears. Well after dark, the crowd began to thin.

Around midnight, Colleen Stansbury, the town's nurse, pulled me on to the porch. "Jonny needs to be cleaned up," she whispered. I followed her to the clinic. A yellow body bag lay on the exam table, zipped tight. Colleen shut off the fluorescent lights and started lighting candles. The room softened in the flicker of a dozen flames.

We each filled a pan with warm water and lifted a stack of cotton swabs from a drawer. We looked at each other over the sealed bag. "Ready?" Colleen asked.

"Yes," I lied.

I could not have done the job alone, could not have found the strength to peel back the zipper and see what remained of my friend. Jon had landed on the back of his head. Falling through twenty feet of open gravity and colliding with frozen ground had crushed his skull and jammed his teeth through his cheek. In the quiet candlelight, I followed Colleen's lead and dipped a corner of cloth into the warm water. As Jon's face came clean, our pans of water grew tinted with red. The right eye, once I had wiped the congealed blood from the socket, was ruptured into a wild cold stare. With cotton swabs, we cleaned the crusted red from his ears. With fresh cloths, we washed the gray slip of brain from his thinning hair.

Colleen stayed with Jon while I drove home. I raided four decks of cards to deal Jon his last cribbage hand: four fives and two jacks, all hearts. Back at the clinic, I fanned the cards on the chest of his wool coat, tucking them under the bib of his rain pants.

I left the clinic and went back to Mary's house. She was still on the couch, eyes wide with shock. It was hard to believe that earlier that same day she'd kissed Jon on her way to work. Surreal to think of Mary coming home and finding Jon curled in the driveway; horrific the thought of Mary touching his shoulder, looking into his shattered face.

I coaxed Mary into the truck, drove to the clinic, and led her into the candle-lit room. She brushed her fingers on Jon's cheek, trying to make sense of the impossible.

———

In the following weeks, Mary rarely slept. Every time she slid toward rest, the image of Jon's broken body bent silently in the driveway flipped her back into terror and shock. Driving to my house one day, Mary saw a body lumped in the road. She put her car in reverse, thinking *I will not do this again. I can't do this again.* When she stopped and looked, the body was gone. She drove forward again, slowly crossing the place where the body never was.

Mary and I spent the coming winter nights whispering around a candle's quiet flame. Although crippled by loss, Mary glowed with a tangible expansiveness, an almost visible light. I returned to Mary's house most every day, both to offer solace but also to make sense of the calm emanating from her grief-stricken being.

"Do you feel what I see?" I asked. "One moment you're crushed and the next you fill the room. You flip from panic to peace. It's horrific and beautiful. What's going on?"

"Hank, this hurts too much to be my own. I sit here in my darkness, and think of all the loss in the world, and I hear an echo: *I am you, I am you*. That's the light. It's a gorgeous sight. If Jonny hadn't died, I'd never see it. How am I supposed to live with that? How can I accept he had to die for me to see this beauty, to know I am so much bigger than myself?"

By Christmas, winter settled in. The sun, somewhere beyond the heavy clouds, dropped into brief, shallow arcs. The snow was steady. At Mary's house, I shoveled the curved path to her door. I grunted each scoop over the shoulder-high berm, finding solace in the rhythm and the weight of the shovel, the cleared line of accomplishment unveiled behind my bent back. The simple work gave a pleasant purpose to days filled with questions.

Why does the most certain outcome of our lives arrive so unexpectedly? Why are we so startled when we encounter death? Every minute, seven thousand humans die on the planet. One hundred thousand deaths in the time it takes to sip a pot of tea. Over a million deaths between each rising of the sun. Consider our fellow vertebrates and all the other forms of life, and uncountable billions of deaths fill each minute. Despite the shock of Jon's fall, death is not a singular event. It is a constant flow.

Inside, clutching a cup of tea, I tried to imagine a billion deaths. Each life a molecule of water, briefly joined to others in a snowflake, floating for a time, swirling down and disappearing into the uniform blanket of white. But Jon, his thick hands and easy laugh, his broken skull and ruptured eye, is not a molecule. The clean imagery of snow cannot obscure the loss. Outside, snow fell through the black night with silent persistence.

———

On a bright March afternoon, Anya and I snapped into our skis and slid into the wide sweep of meadow. Fresh snow threw a million sparks back at the sun. We skied through the neighborhood to the road's end and cut a fresh trail toward the crane flats. Deep tracks of moose wandered from bush to bush. A wolf winding south and a marten loping west left lines of light, wide prints.

The hiss of skis and huff of breath formed a tight cloud of sound that followed us across the frozen wetlands. We stopped amid an open expanse—the place where cranes would soon land. The white teeth of mountains scraped the horizon in all directions. The high twitter of a flock of siskins, a raven call from the beach, and then silence so wide it carried an echo. We stood shoulder to shoulder, leaning on our poles. I swallowed a lump the size of a cantaloupe. "Anya, will you marry me?"

Anya's round eyes pooled with tears. "Of course," she whispered.

The courage to step into marriage was a gift from Jonny, passed through Mary. "I have no regrets," Mary told me one night. "I know I loved him well. He is gone forever, but I'll always know I held nothing back."

When Mary spoke at our wedding, her words were rich with the truth of grief. She spoke not just of survival but of liberation. She described finding Jon in the driveway and how that experience filled her existence with the refrain *life is short, life is short, life is short*. "I offer these words as a gift," said Mary. "As a lesson not learned the hard way. The worst possible thing that could happen to me happened—there is not much I fear anymore. There is great comfort in savoring every moment we spend together. The inevitable good-byes come so much easier if we have loved as much as we could love."

Lunch Meat and the Pimentos was a band of aging hippies with a repertoire of old rock and roll tunes. Their wedding policy was to play until musicians outnumbered dancers. They started with a traditional waltz. Anya and I alone spun circles in the circle of our friends. The pace quickened and our friends flooded the floor. At midnight neither the band nor the dancers showed any signs of slowing. Anya and I bowed, leaped, spun, and jiggled, celebrating the ephemeral gift of togetherness, in a flock of laughing, sweating humans.

Chapter Eleven

CARIBOU AND CATHOLICS

THE DAY GEORGE BUSH WAS PLACED IN OFFICE, I split a cord of wood. After hearing the news, I turned off the radio and sat alone in the still house. Restless, I strapped on a headlamp and slipped on a wool coat. The creek gurgled through the dark as I made my way across the meadow to the hill of unsplit wood piled in the driveway. A light freezing rain coated the maul handle with a slick layer of ice. I waited for the heat of my hands to melt through to the familiar grip of wood. I centered a round on the chopping block in the feeble beam of light. Round after round cleaved beneath the maul. I swung with a steadiness that made my heart pound and sweat tickle my ribs. I stripped to a t shirt and kept swinging. After a few hours, the batteries started to fade. I kept swinging until my light went out completely and then stood, letting the cold night close in.

Within days, Bush's corporate cronies were rubbing their hands, plotting to put oil rigs in the Arctic National Wildlife Refuge. The Refuge is well outside my home range; I have never been there and will likely never go. I know the northern tundra and Arctic mountains are beautiful, but so are the coves, valleys, peaks, and glaciers surrounding my rainforest home. If I had known it was going to be just one oil rig, just one industrial complex, I might not have cared. But the eagerness to tear up public ground for private profit was not going to stop in the

Arctic. I feared for Frank's Mountain, for Lemesurier Island, for my personal piece of the public pie.

I called my friend Carolyn Servid in Sitka, a hundred miles to the south. Her voice, like mine, was heavy, devoid of music. Like me, she had never been to the Refuge, but if Bush was starting with the Arctic, we would too. A few days later, Carolyn and I mailed an invitation to over fifty writers, scientists, historians, poets, and politicians—asking for a piece of writing in defense of the Arctic National Wildlife Refuge. We had no publisher, no funding, no solid plan, only the irresistible need to do something, anything. Within weeks, we received more poems, essays, and heartfelt testimonies than we could ever publish in a single volume.

Two months, a few hundred phone calls, and countless emails later, I was on my way to the halls of the U.S. Congress. Before I left, Kim stopped by with a stack of freshly printed business cards. "They're kinda like suits and ties," Kim explained. "Everybody back there has these things."

Hank Lentfer—Lip Flapper Extraordinaire, the card read. Centered above my contact information was the question: *What is the sound of one lip flapping?*

"You're going to need them," Kim assured me. "People back there stopped laughing a long time ago."

Fellow writers Bill McKibben, Richard Nelson, Scott Russell Sanders, and Sarah James made the trip with me. We gathered in Senator John Kerry's office for a press conference announcing the publication of *Arctic Refuge: A Circle of Testimony.* We hung out in the dark paneled room eating bagels and cream cheese and waiting for Kerry—who was, of course, late. I snitched another piece of smoked salmon and a clump of grapes while I studied a high wall covered with pictures of Kerry shaking hands with American and foreign leaders. Many Alaskans kill the biggest animals they can find and mount each head on a wall. Senators, it seemed, made trophies of their proximity to power.

When Kerry finally whisked into the room the camera lights flipped on. I carefully wiped the cream cheese from my mustache before presenting him with a copy of the book. Sarah James gave him a small stuffed caribou. Kerry stared into the camera, pounded the table, and pledged his defense of America's "Great Refuge." Ten minutes and a few handshakes later he was gone. I grabbed a couple of cookies as the camera crew packed up.

I stayed in Washington for a week with fellow Alaskan Richard Nelson, running from one senate office to the next, handing out our little book. We got lost between each appointment. "You'd think a couple of Alaska outdoor buffs could figure out where they're going," Richard said as we ran up a wide flight of marbled steps two at a time.

"No way," I said between breaths. "At home there are mountains, trees, and sun. Everything in here looks the same."

Late for yet another appointment, we decided to take the elevator. We joined a throng of suited men and pointy-shoed women waiting before a row of closed doors. An elevator marked SENATORS ONLY opened, but nobody moved.

"C'mon," I whispered to Richard. We entered the empty elevator and turned to see dozens of astonished faces.

"Hey!" someone shouted. "You can't do that!"

"Senator Lentfer," I said as the doors slid shut. "Appreciate your vote."

Other days, I tagged along with Sarah James. Her Athabascan features and thick accent blew an authentic air through her testimony. "We just want the caribou to keep coming," she explained in each office. "We have seen oil money destroy other villages. We don't want money. We just want our way of life." Each senate staffer listened with forced attentiveness. Some even took notes.

"I don't think these people are really listening," Sarah confided after a dozen visits.

"Well, it's not every day someone asks to stop the flow of money," I said. "It just doesn't compute. We might as well be in the Vatican trying to convince the pope Jesus was a bonehead."

———

By a two-vote margin, the Senate rejected the president's pro-drilling agenda. But the showdown was far from over. In a stream of podium-pounding speeches, politicians described the Refuge as everything from a bleak wasteland to the American Serengeti. Determined to do my part, I made trip after trip. Kim filled a slide carousel of his best Arctic images. I took the photos and a box of books to the home states of on-the-fence senators. Night after night, I showed the pictures and made my plea, urging people to write to their elected officials.

Driving from Chicago's O'Hare airport into northern Indiana, I encountered my first tollbooth. I pulled my rental car to the shortest line and stopped behind a shiny gold Oldsmobile. My eye was immediately drawn to the one bumper sticker on the otherwise unblemished car. The blue-and-white swirled marble of Earth in space hung on a white background. I don't recall what I expected the words to convey—maybe "World Peace," or "One Planet, One People," or "We Are All One." Whatever my expectations, they left no room for the five words printed in bold green alongside our spinning planet: "This Is Not MY Home." The sticker pulled away, leaving a fading breath of exhaust. I dutifully eased forward to pay my buck fifteen to the impatient attendant.

My first stop in Indiana was the University of Notre Dame. I met up with Nikki, the student president of the campus conservation group (membership of five). With Nikki's help, I set out brochures and poster-sized pictures of the Refuge on a table in the cafeteria. Occasionally someone eddied out of the river of hungry, book-toting students to see what we were about. While a few students asked questions and picked up a pamphlet, most turned up their noses and stomped off with indignant, even angry, snorts. After a few dozen snorts, Nikki noticed my surprise.

"Welcome to the Bible Belt, Hank." Nikki went on to explain that campus politics among the Catholic student body revolved around abortion. The Arctic National Wildlife Refuge was obviously a Democratic issue—therefore I must be a baby killer and deserving of a good searing snort.

"Seems like the Bible Belt needs to loosen up a notch."

"Yeah, right," said Nikki. "In your dreams."

Leaving Notre Dame the next morning, I drove the length of the state through rolling gray fields of corn stubble. I pulled into Bloomington in late afternoon and followed directions to the home of Scott and Ruth Sanders, the only people I knew in the state. I had not seen Scott since our time together in Senator Kerry's office. His broad smiling face and Ruth's quiet warmth were welcome after the cold Notre Dame reception.

Every day for the next week, Scott and I drove to some corner of Indiana to perform our song and dance about the Arctic's beauty and the desperate need for restraint. Born and raised in the Bible Belt, Scott knew his audience. Quoting scripture from memory, he made a convincing case that God Himself was a conservationist. Scott opened each evening by reminding folks that "wilderness represents in space what the Sabbath represents in time—a limit to our dominion, a refuge from the quest for power and wealth, an acknowledgment that the earth does not belong to us."

To an audience gathered in a church not far from the Indianapolis 500 speedway, Scott asked, "If the Lord quit shaping the earth after six days, looked at what had been made, and saw that it was very good, then who are we to keep shaping the earth for all seven days?" I showed Kim's photos of migrating caribou strung across the tundra like strands of a vibrant, living web; Dall sheep perched on snow-capped cliffs; long-haired musk oxen circled like Pleistocene relics. I spoke about the wheeling magic of cranes and the myriad species that gather to nest in the brief Arctic summer.

A young man from a back pew raised his hand. "I hear the footprint of a drilling pad would only take up a fraction of a percent of ANWR. It would be nice to leave it alone, but we have to have jobs."

"Imagine someone drawing a razor across the face of the Mona Lisa," I said. "Only a fraction of the canvas would be touched."

"If it is true," Scott added, "that our economy will fail unless we devote every minute and every acre to the pursuit of profit, then our economy is already doomed. For where shall we turn after the calendar and the continent have been exhausted?"

Our last evening of the Indiana Tour was spent with the Sisters of Saint Mary-of-the-Woods. Driving the winding, tree-lined lane through the sprawling convent, I was surprised to see women tending gardens in jeans and sweaters. We parked in front of a high, stone church. Two women, clad in skirts and blouses, walked down the wide steps.

"I was expecting penguin suits," I said.

"I think these sisters are bit more progressive than that," Scott answered.

The three dozen gray-haired nuns who gathered for our presentation were, by far, our most receptive audience.

"What sort of religion do politicians follow," Scott asked, "if it places no limits on human dominion? What sort of religion do they follow if it makes the pursuit of profit the central goal of life?" All fifty gray heads nodded in agreement as Scott continued. "If politicians believe in keeping the Sabbath holy, how can they reconcile this commandment with the drive to reduce every acre and every hour to human control?"

Throughout the slideshow the nuns responded to each image with murmurs of appreciation. They had, I am sure, much in common with the young Catholics on the campus of Notre Dame. But their lives seemed unpolluted by politics. They recognized the impulse to protect a newborn human and an ancient crane as one and the same. I clicked through Kim's pictures, smiling in the dark, happy to share a room with people with such a tangible love of life.

None of those women were likely to make the journey to the Arctic, but as soon as Scott and I finished, pens and paper were distributed and the Sisters of Saint Mary-of-the-Woods fell to the task of letting Indiana senator Richard Lugar know that the distant stretch of tundra was, indeed, part of their home—and deserving of their care.

———

In the years before Bush's presidency I rarely left the yard, much less the state. Within months of the inauguration, I was well on my way to earning MVP status on Alaska Airlines. While packing my bags for yet another trip, a small flock of cranes passed low over our house, tree tops almost scratching their gray bellies. That close, the high peeps of young cranes rang clear. Barely three months old, those birds followed their parents with no thought of the return journey or the oil pooled deep beneath their nesting grounds. I watched the cranes disappear to the south before driving myself to the airport. The cranes were following the same urge that had led their species through millions of years. I boarded the tubular confines of a jet, a mode of travel unimaginable in my grandfather's youth. If the cranes were led by faith, I was pushed by fear.

My first reading was in Seattle. I met my friend and musician Libby Roderick for lunch. It was September 11, 2001. Dazed by the morning's images of crumbling towers, we found little appetite for conversation or calories. In a daze we wandered the semideserted downtown streets. That evening, a dozen equally stunned folks joined us in the windowless basement of the Elliot Bay Bookstore. We quickly abandoned the podium and circled the chairs. With the help of Libby's guitar and clear voice, talk of politics soon gave way to song, and then a circle of hands and silence.

In Portland, several days and many readings later, the magnitude of the attacks suddenly penetrated my protective numbness. It was a Sunday. I had just finished digesting the morning paper's report of inevitable unrest in the Middle East, soaring gas prices, the need for heightened national security. Surely the U.S. Senate would vote to pull oil from the Arctic Refuge to fuel the impending war. I was overcome with vivid images of the rubble from New York billowing all the way to the Arctic coastal plain, of cranes flying through dust that would not settle, birds endlessly circling, unable to find their breeding grounds.

My hope was stripped by the reality that there is no place remote enough—not even in Alaska—to be free of the violence of human greed and aggression. My tears were for the cranes, for the silence draining from Lemesurier Island, for the peace unborn children would not know. Working to protect a sliver of Arctic coastline was a futile, puny task in a world gone mad.

The talking heads on the airport televisions yammered about how the attacks on the Twin Towers changed the world. Watching the buildings fall for the hundredth time, I thought of Joseph Stalin's words: *One death is a tragedy; a million deaths is a statistic.* Stalin went on to craft policies that starved ten million peasants. Another ten million died in purges and gulags. Pol Pot killed two million of his fellow Cambodians. A million Irish men, women, and children starved under the constraints of English policy. Mao's Great Leap Forward claimed the lives of thirty million Chinese. Eight hundred thousand Tutsis were killed by machetes in less than one hundred days. Under U.S. sanctions, five hundred thousand Iraqi children died of malnutrition and disease. One hundred years before my birth, seven hundred thousand men were shredded by musket rounds and cannon fodder in the American Civil War. Ten thousand Native Americans died along the Trail of Tears, just one of a thousand forced marches.

The talking heads were wrong. All that had changed was the ability of modern Americans to maintain the delusion that we are somehow immune from the violent reach of history. The tear-stained faces of people holding candles around the perimeter of the rubble were the newest take on an old tragedy.

I remember little of what I said to the small groups gathered in bookstores in the weeks following 9/11; the horrors of history spilling into a future of our own making swept away any words of hope. One woman told me she started painting when the towers came down and could not stop; the backs of her hands were speckled with color. A man my own age lingered one evening, approaching me after the others had left.

"What do you do if your work makes no difference?" he asked. "What do you do if no one listens?"

I wanted to say, *Don't worry, they will listen. Don't worry, our leaders are truly wise. Don't worry, compassion is more powerful than revenge.* I wanted to hear myself say something hopeful, but I was too tired to be dishonest.

"I don't know," I said. "I really don't know."

I traveled home through airports gripped in distrust. By the time I was walking the familiar path across the quiet meadow, I felt as though I'd been away for years, not weeks. When the last flock of cranes passed over, I lay on my back and stared up into the swirling sea of birds. I closed my eyes. No matter how intently I listened, their voices seemed unchanged. Why did one presidential election throw me into a depression? How did people convince themselves the earth is not our home? Why did people believe one act of violence in New York actually changed the world? What would happen if all Christian sermons and each Islamic call to prayer, every Senate testimonial and every newscast around the planet, were replaced, for just twenty-four hours, with the sound of migrating cranes?

Chapter Twelve

LETTER TO AN UNBORN CHILD

THE CLOSER I CAME TO FATHERHOOD, the harder I worked to get away. I imagined a child deciphering the world of language only to hear newscasters tell of the latest death tolls. I imagined the love of a field being buried beneath the convenience of asphalt. I imagined the chorus of cranes being swallowed by an empty sky.

The question of parenthood, however, was not really up to me. My life was entwined with a woman whose idea of a good time was to hang out in the baby clothes section of the Salvation Army store. Anya sought out newborns in airports and parking lots. She'd lift a crying infant from a stranger's arms and bounce it into silence before handing it back to the grateful mother. Anya became a physician so she could witness baby after baby entering the world. I was too naive to see that doctoring was merely an orbit around motherhood. No number of babies passing through her hands could fill the urge to pass one through her body.

Anya listened with sincerity to my guilt about adding a child to a planet already groaning with each human birth. She considered, without laughing, my suggestion that we fill our parental urges by spending a little more time with the neighbor boy. One night after dinner I shared my latest list of reasons. "Ice caps are melting. Oceans are rising. By the time our kid turns fifty there will be nine billion humans on the planet all fighting for a clean glass of water. The nightmare of the American dream is circling the globe like an unstoppable virus. Clear-cuts are spreading like a fungus. I don't want to expose a kid to all that."

Anya wisely offered no rebuttals. She just looked up from her knitting and nodded. I pretended not to notice the project hanging from her needles was a baby-sized sweater.

I took the question of fatherhood to Lemesurier. It was near Christmas; Bob was visiting family in Seattle, Anya working in Juneau. The long evenings passed in slow solitude. I spent the short days with the raucous crows and silent deer. After a week, I came home with this letter written to an unborn child:

———

I have come to the place I wish to be buried. The trail winding steeply through the forest is marked here and there with tufts of hair pulled from the hides of deer I dragged to the beach earlier this fall. The weight of their bodies gives the path a swept look, like someone has tidied up with a broom. The trail holds years of stories and the promise of memories as yet unmade; hikes and hunts in summer sun and winter snow; days spent with my closest friends and the woman who is to be your mother.

Today I walk it alone. It is mid-December. The rain on the beach cools to slush as I gain elevation. The muskeg, at 500 feet, is covered by a thin layer of heavy snow crossed by the prints of deer.

I have come here because it is the place where prayers live. I see them in the tracks of deer, hear them in the whistle of wind through raven wings, sense them in the black depths of a hidden lake.

My education in biology gives me images of sperm and egg, cells dividing and differentiating day by day into familiar human-oid shapes. But where are you now, before the cellular unfolding in your mother's belly? Where are you as I wrestle with the questions of fatherhood? I want to talk with you. I want to share my fears. I want to uncover my joy. I know of course that words themselves, scratched on to this rain-blotted page, cannot reach you.

If there is a way to speak to you I am guessing it revolves around the language of prayer; not a specific recitation, but simply a place of open heart. I have brought a tool, wrapped in soft deer leather, to help work through the tangle of thoughts that crowd the openness I seek. It is a pipe cut from the arc of an antler. The carved bowl is burnt black. The smooth curve rests lightly in my hand.

For years I have gathered bits of deer food from each place an animal fell: the thick leaves of bunchberry, finely toothed trailing blackberry, the intricate shape of fine-leafed gold thread. I dry the leaves near the woodstove and add them to the pouch that travels with my pipe. Now, seated beneath the sheltering arms of an old spruce, I dip my fingers into the pouch, reaching for the first prayer. The leaves crack and crumble between my fingers.

A prayer for sorrow. The world seems so inextricably wrapped in loss. The longer I live and the more I love, the greater the sadness that will flood my days as I bury my parents, my friends, sweet Anya. I have come to understand there are lessons hidden in each passing so I don't fear the losses as much as I once did. Thinking of you, however, I feel a new pain at knowing the losses that will sting your days as surely as the salty sea. Already I want to shield you from the lineage of loss, the river of hurt flowing your way. Perhaps we together or you alone will carry your mother's ashes to the mountain top where the bones of her father have long since fused back to earth.

You will, most likely, help lug my cold and stiff body back to this place. I hope disease or age has withered my flesh to a husk to lighten your load. I hope there is a circle of friends to share the burden. Drag me if you must. Sweep the trail the other way. Let the deer walk where my body has been. I hope it is summer, the ground soft, the sky clear.

You may, as I have, find your heart broken by love of a cove or creek, forest or fen that you later see destroyed by the hand of human greed. Such loss leaves me battling with a swelling bitterness that masks the world's beauty as darkly as asphalt itself. I wish you places beautiful enough to invoke your love and the wisdom to weather its change. No matter how great the loss, may you never lose sight of the beauty that remains.

A prayer for tears. May you find the courage to let them flow, to relax against the tendency to hold on to pain. Tears open the heart, blurring bitterness, dissolving anger, healing hurt.

A prayer for joy, the kind that bursts when the unexpected happens right on cue—the deer who just now stepped past my perch, a buck in his prime, deep tan antlers in graceful pointed curves, black nose twitching. The deer caught my dangerous scent and strutted off on stiff legs, tail raised. He had no way of knowing that today I carry no rifle, that I come only with thoughts of your birth. I hope you learn from the wisdom of deer who know clearest of all there is no difference between death and creation.

A prayer for mystery. I do not know where you are and I don't know anyone who does. Nowhere? Everywhere? One answer is as good as the next. I like not knowing; it leaves so much room for the possible. I have heard stories, had dreams, known the chill of eerie experience which all speaks to the existence of worlds parallel to the one I daily probe with sight and sound. The existence of multiple realities is no more startling than the presence of any at all. I love to dabble in mysterious places and dream of ripples that know no shore. I like the invisible force that ties me, already, to wherever you are.

A prayer for place. If you choose to come into our lives you will be born into a place of abundance and peace. On this curve of the earth the land is thick with life. The trees hold memories of centuries, the moss lies deep like a continuous featherbed. The waters are full too. All summer, salmon leap like silver needles and whales roll their slow arched backs. You will not know hunger. Food is easily gathered from all that walks, swims, flies and grows in this rain-soaked land. Scarcity is a word born in distant lands.

Your home will know no boundaries. Your body will know the curves of creeks, reach of trees, and calls of cranes. You will know, as surely as the warmth of Anya's arms, the earth holds you and offers all you need. It is, for now, a place free of war and violence. You will find no locked doors, ours or the neighbors'. A bike and fishing pole and the wide stretch of summer are yours. I will do what I can to keep such peace unbroken.

A prayer for play. This fall, on this island, on a rare day of sun, I played a long game of kick ball. A group of boys, ages twelve to forty-five, picked teams, debated the bases, settling on a tree for first, a rotten wooden boat for second, a mossed over stump for third, and a sweatshirt for home plate. We kicked, ran, slid, and tumbled for half a sweaty day. Our whoops of laughter rang through the valley, mixing with the calls of geese winging their way south. May play never leave your days. May your tears be answered with laughter.

A prayer for gratitude. Gratitude is the pool in which all good things gather. It is the combined state of acceptance and humility, awareness and faith, joy and sorrow, compassion and caring. It resonates through an open heart like a finely tuned guitar.

I am grateful the oldest bird on the planet transforms the sky above my home into an amphitheater of sound. Grateful to share trails and berry patches with bears. Grateful for streams still vibrant with the annual return of salmon.

Today I am grateful for the deer who have stood still in the face of death; grateful that I will be buried where the roots of plants can nibble *at my flesh and offer my body back to the deer; grateful to share my days with a woman who loves this place and who loves me as much as she already loves you; grateful for the circle of friends who radiate warmth into my life and into whose blanket you are invited; grateful to watch the turn of another season; grateful for the chance to know you; grateful for gratitude itself.*

A prayer for love. Next month Anya and I will head to the coast of the open ocean to camp where winter storms tug at the roots of trees and shape rock with crashing tongues of water. There, in love, we will invite you into our lives. If you come, it will be in love that you live.

The pipe is full. I hold a flame to the lip of the blackened bowl and pull the flickering fire with my breath. Smoke rushes warm on the back of my throat. Each in-breath brings a hushed crackle of fire. The smoke rises dense around my head, ghost forms dancing before they vanish to wherever it is they go. The antler slowly warms to hot. Breath, fire, and prayer merge into ash and silence. With cupped hands I hold the cooling heat. Chickadees chatter at the edge of hearing. A raven calls. Another answers.

Chapter Thirteen

SPIN IT DOWN

MY RELUCTANCE TO ACCEPT FATHERHOOD slipped away after the first miscarriage. Six months later, our hopes took flight with another positive pregnancy test. Those hopes soon crashed, and Anya and I buried the bloody stretch of tissue from the second miscarriage alongside the first underneath a young hemlock tree behind the house. There is a fierce privacy in mourning the loss of the faceless unborn. It is a grief without texture or weight, the absence of air for lungs that never existed.

For a year, Anya did not conceive again. Nothing happened. Each month we teetered between anticipation and disappointment. As we neared Anya's fortieth birthday, her biological clock escalated into a shrill bell. Romance and candles were replaced by calendars and thermometers. Anya finally lost patience and asked a fellow doctor, Lindy Jones, for help. The next thing I knew, another man was helping me impregnate my wife.

After decades of birth control, trying to make a baby should be a wildly out-of-control experience. It should be the orgasm of a lifetime, the true alignment with the cosmic flow, the moment my two-hundred-pound, hormone-addled, sperm-delivery-system-of-a-body was born to fulfill. The lab's bright lights and sterile counters were a world away from the wild beach where I'd imagined conceiving our child.

At least Anya had a key to the clinic so we could do our technological tinkering in the privacy of late evening. Following Dr. Jones's instructions, we dutifully showed up with a plastic container holding a mix of my sperm and the contents of a little glass bottle marked "bovine serum." I was not crazy about mixing my seed with cow juice but Anya assured me Lindy knew what he was doing.

Lindy filled a test tube, placed it in a centrifuge, clicked the lid shut, and set the timer for ten minutes. The little machine whirred to life with a precise hum. When the centrifuge slowed to a stop, Lindy lifted the tube to the light. We all peered at the white pellet balled in the round bottom. "There they are," Lindy said proudly, as if it were his own off-spring. "A half a million wannabe babies in that little ball."

"I bet they're dizzy," I said.

Lindy took a syringe and delicately sucked up a drop of fluid near the pellet's edge. He spread the sample on a glass slide, handed the test tube to me, and then fiddled with a microscope. "Take a look at this," Lindy said. Squinting through the twin eyepieces, my gaze fell through a world of motion: frantically whipping tails propelling egg-shaped bodies in all directions. They wriggled on and off stage with great, straight-lined determination. It was eerily quiet down there. There should be sound effects, I thought: honking, buzzing, helicopter noise, something.

"Oops, there's one curving to the left," I said.

"Probably a liberal," commented Lindy.

Satisfied that at least some sperm were still swimming straight after their wild spin, Lindy sucked the entire white pellet into a fresh syringe. We went from lab room to exam room where my wife, without fanfare, shucked her pants and settled into the stirrups. Lindy fitted the speculum and adjusted lights to bring the target into view. Following his instructions, I tore the sterile packaging from a ten-inch flexible tube no thicker than pencil lead.

With gloved hand, Lindy fit the tube onto the syringe and eased the end through the tiny hole of Anya's cervix. A quick squeeze on the plunger and it was over. "Wow, you're quick," I said.

"Direct deposit. The race is on in there," Lindy replied.

"You want a cigarette or anything?"

"How about a cigar when one of those things turns into a full-on baby?" Lindy suggested.

We waited three long weeks to see if Lindy's trick worked. When the test came back positive, we didn't tell anyone, barely talked about it ourselves. After two miscarriages, we were afraid to be hopeful. A few months later, we made a midnight run to Anya's clinic. Sneaking through the darkened halls, we flipped on the lights in an exam room crowded with keyboards, cords, and computer screens. Anya fired up the ultrasound, settled back on the table, and slid a gizmo across her belly. Anya's trained eyes made sense of the monitor's swirling gray blur.

"There are the chambers of the heart. There's the head. See the reflection of the eye?"

"Nope, all I see is pure fuzziness."

"Here, listen to this." Anya reached out, tapped a few keys, and the small room filled with the sound of a tiny heart thumping along at a steady one hundred and forty beats per minute.

———

A raven's squawk filled my ears when I answered the phone.

"What do you want, Kim?"

"Bike ride? Ice cream?" he asked.

"Sure."

It was sunny—a rarity in fall. We pedaled down the center of the quiet pavement, swerving around the dotted yellow lines as though skiing a slalom course. We skidded to a stop before the Beartrack Mercantile, the town's one general store. I bought a lime Popsicle. Kim grabbed an ice cream sandwich. We joined a gaggle of neighbors and a few visitors lounging on the porch swing and leaning against dusty trucks. Buoyed by the sun, the banter was quick and light, peppered with laughter. We heard the cranes moments before they poured into view. Hundreds of birds, winging just above the treetops, sprayed the parking lot with shadow and song. Not until they passed, pulling their blanket of sound with them, did I realize everyone was silent. A visiting fisherman in camo pants broke the quiet. "Goddamn, that was something. What the hell were they?"

"Those are the reasons we live here," answered Kim, biting the corner off his ice cream bar.

Why is it that people deaf to the waterfall song of a winter wren or blind to the acrobatics of a raven can be struck dumb by the sound of cranes? The Greek word for a crane chorus is *inangling*. The Koyukun people of Alaska call sandhills *dildoola,* in mimicry of their call. Aldo Leopold described the sounds of approaching sandhills as the "tinkling of little bells," the "baying of some sweet-throated hound," and a "pandemonium of trumpets, rattles, croaks, and cries." The ornithologist Scott Weidensaul describes the sound of a far-off flock as "fingernails drawn along the teeth of several combs, but with a rich melodic sound, like delicate bamboo chimes struck with small mallets." My friend Jen says it's the ghost of an owl playing a wooden flute.

Sandhills are the loudest birds in the world. Their resonance and volume comes through a trachea that doubles back on itself in a tightly curved S-shape fused to the chest bone. Stretched out, the windpipe is longer than the bird itself. Bony rings in this elongated tube make the whole apparatus vibrate during vocalization, amplifying and adding complex harmonics. The sound carries for miles. On still days, I have heard the faint whisper of far-off cranes winging through a blue sky beyond the edge of sight. At tree-top level, the sound of kettling cranes crescendos through my ears and reverberates against my chest.

I too am at a loss to pin the depth of sound onto the flat page. To me the fall chorus is the sound of an irresistible smile, the corners of my mouth and threads of cranes pulled by a common force. Not until I heard the thrumming of my child's heart did I feel a smile tugged into existence in quite the same way.

Chapter Fourteen

CONDOS AND CORN

SECOND CUP OF COFFEE, woodstove just easing back the early morning chill, breakfast hot on the table. After two bites Anya set down her spoon, closed her eyes, then bolted for the door. She came back, wiping the corners of her mouth.

"Hardly seems right," I said, "that a creature needing you to eat makes you blow your oatmeal every morning."

"Just means the little bugger is getting serious about sticking around this time." Anya sat back at the table, nibbled an apple slice.

"You mind if I eat your oats before they get cold?"

"All yours," Anya said, pushing the bowl across the table. "I don't even want to look at it." I slurped down my second bowl of cereal while flipping through Anya's embryology text. A color photo of a three-month fetus revealed a massive bulbous forehead dwarfing the scrawny beginnings of humanoid limbs. The author, for some twisted reason, placed a picture of a fetal pig alongside the human baby. Both critters had stubby tails, one yet to be absorbed, the other yet to twist into a tight curl. Both were round and swollen like overstuffed manatees or pale pollywogs. Both showed the faint lines of recently closed gill slits.

"It's a good thing we can't see our kids until they look like us," I told Anya. "Not sure I could learn to love a puffy little pig."

"At least pregnant pigs don't puke," Anya said.

At birth, there are over one hundred billion neurons in the human brain produced at a rate of two hundred fifty thousand per minute throughout the nine months of gestation. When a child comes into the world, this vast potential is largely untapped; it's like an international system of telephones installed but not hooked up. The neurological hook up ("synaptogenesis," says the textbook) takes place through the first two years of life. At its peak, fifteen thousand synapses are produced on each neuron: 1.8 million new hookups per second, nonstop, for a couple of years. While these billions of nerves are busy linking up with their neighbors, the child remains alarmingly helpless.

Pigs, when they are born, find their way to a nipple and get right to the business of being a pig. Deer stand and wobble after their mothers within an hour of emerging from the womb. Crane chicks snap at bugs days out of the egg and fly two thousand miles a few months later. Human babies spastically squirm for months before they can even roll over. For years they have to be lifted to the nipple and carried from place to place. Stinking diapers and sleepless nights are the price our parents pay for our big brains.

Individually, it works. Given even semiattentive parents, babies grow into wildly successful creatures: masters of manipulation, able to run, swim, climb, fly, and order Chinese take-out all in the same day. Collectively, it's too early to tell if banking on our multibillion bundles of brain cells is a good bet. No doubt our big brains get us into trouble. No answers yet as to whether they are big enough to get us out.

————

Cranes will likely survive the dwindling decades of my life. After hearing that tiny heartbeat fill the exam room, I needed to know about the chances of cranes surviving the century of my child's life. I'd called Mike Eaton as a stranger, just introduced myself and started asking questions about the cranes I knew lived near his home in California. Before I hung up, I had four pages of notes and an invitation to come and stay. It takes cranes weeks to the make the trip to California. In a window seat on an Alaska Airlines jet, it took me ten hours. Watching the intricate islands of the West Coast slip beneath the aluminum shell of the plane, I tried to imagine having nothing but feathers between me and all that open space, the whistle of wind through long primaries, the voices of mate and off-spring calling behind outstretched legs.

Dropping through ten thousand feet on the descent to Sacramento, I studied the swatches and strips of agriculture yielding to the wide sweep of slow rivers; a pastoral landscape designed by surveyors and textured by farmers. After the bustle of the airport and the frenzy of the freeway, the quiet of Mike's house was a welcome refuge. Mike and his wife, Charity, had recently built their home on the edge of the preserve they helped create. They were quintessential conservationists: bright, dedicated, motivated by a love for birds. An electric car crowded the carport along-side a new hybrid. Raised garden boxes at the end of the house sported a growth of wintergreens. The gift of smoked salmon I brought from Alaska remained uneaten in a refrigerator filled with vegetarian cuisine.

The house faced a field sloping to the banks of the Consumnes River where a band of wild turkeys plucked their way toward a stand of oaks. Around back, rows of leafless grape vines hung silent beneath the tepid winter sun. Just past Mike and Charity's house, the gravel drive-way morphed into a muddy trail winding through a cattail swamp. Mal-lards, pintails, and coots flushed from the ponds. I sat on an old car seat, the central feature of some hunter's duck blind. I listened for cranes but heard only the hum of highways and the high whistle of jets.

Back at the house I dug through Mike's extensive library. I learned the luxuriant oak savanna and sprawling complex of wetlands that first attracted cranes to California's Central Valley is now relegated to the stories of indigenous people and the journal pages of early pioneers. Displaced are the three hundred thousand Native Americans once belonging to fifty tribes. Gone are the vast herds of tulle elk, the brown bear, and the wolf. Diminished is the diversity of the native habitats now growing rows of condos and corn. Drained are six million acres of once widespread wetlands. Starting with an initial purchase of eighty-four acres of remnant oak forest, the Consumnes Preserve has grown to forty-five thousand acres of wetlands, riparian forests, grasslands, and grain-based crops grown for the benefit of cranes and waterfowl. The land is owned and managed by a mix of federal, state, and county agencies, as well as conservation groups, cattle ranchers, corn and rice farmers, and duck hunters. Drawn by a common love of birds, these oddball partners buy land, negotiate easements, and do whatever they can to carve a little space for cranes.

———

Everyone knows that water flows downhill; that's why rivers cut channels below the surrounding landscape. The pattern is reversed in the braided waterways where the Sacramento and San Joaquin rivers merge in the Central Valley. Each strand of winding river is pinched in place by hills of mounded dirt. The fight against physics started in the 1930s, when wheat farmers began building up the rivers' banks to protect their crops from seasonal floods. Dust billowing behind plows lowered the fields, and each year the levees were pushed a bit higher. Now the croplands are a full twenty feet below river level. What used to be an extensive flood-prone tulle swamp is now partitioned into flat-bottomed, shallow bowls filled with corn and asparagus. Local farmers refer to the complex of levees, croplands, and stranded channels as "the delta."

Brent Tadman is the manager of Staten Island, a nine-thousand-acre cornfield on the delta. Typical of farmers, he wears a stained, curled cowboy hat and denim jacket. Atypical is the Nature Conservancy logo barely visible beneath the dust caked on the door of his pickup.

"This is a working farm," Brent explained. "It has to pay for itself. But along the way we do what we can for the cranes."

Driving the ruts on the levee top, Brent points out the huge pumps required to remove water continuously seeping through the dirt levees. Brent stops the lurching truck near a group of two hundred cranes feeding through the corn stubble. "We push up micro levees and flood part of the field so they have a place to roost. We got million-dollar pumps to get the water out and then we go ahead and spill it back in."

Brent watched the feeding cranes in silence. "I'm just a farmer, but you can't help but love these birds. Compared to them, our life spans ain't spit. They been flying through time. Wish they'd a taken a few notes along the way."

Like all farmers on the delta, Brent's greatest struggle is water management—too much in spring, not enough in summer. Brent showed me a stretch of steel sheet piling used to stop a leak.

"This was a $600,000 patch job," he said, shaking his head. "Snowmelt last spring caused it. Had my guys patrolling twenty-four hours a day. Caught this one early. Fella on the next island over had a full breach. Started out the size of a truck. By the time they returned with some rock it was two hundred yards wide." Brent shut off the engine and passed his gaze from the river to the birds. "Cost those guys over $100 million to fix that hole. You got to sell a goddamn lot of corn to make that pay."

In the summer, there is not enough water. An open-air aqueduct siphons the water from the two river systems to quench the ever-growing thirst of millions in the L.A. basin. The diverted fresh water is replaced by water from the sea. "Not only are we below river level," Brent explained, "but we are below sea level. The flow of fresh water is the only thing keeping the sea from poisoning our fields with salt. When it comes to a pissing match between swimming pools and roosting cranes, guess who's gonna lose."

We got out of the truck and walked the river's edge. Below us, wary cranes slowly skulked away. A speedboat careened past, heading upstream; its wake sloshed onto the dirt road.

"This place is just like New Orleans," Brent said, kicking a rock into the river. "Except here, when the levees go it'll be cranes, corn, and a handful of farmers that get drowned out. No one even knows we're here. Don't reckon they'll notice when we're gone."

Keith Whitener, manager of the Consumnes Preserve, is a high-energy, keenly intelligent man typical of Nature Conservancy administrators. While ducks paddle through the wetlands outside his office window, Keith wades through the piles of emails and phone messages required to coordinate the diverse partners of the Consumnes Project. With a squirrel's nervous precision, Keith works through a mouthful of sunflower seeds while answering my questions. I ask his prediction of the sandhill cranes' future.

"We've got five, maybe ten years left to broker a few more land deals, then the lines between development and protection will all be drawn." He spit a shell into the wastebasket. "After that it'll be up to the cranes to survive with what scraps are left."

———

A friend told me that parenthood is like having your heart race around outside your body. His children were teenagers. Good kids, but still teenagers. "Parenting, from the get-go," my friend said, "is one long lesson in letting go of what was never yours."

I spent my last hours in California strolling along a boardwalk through a federally managed wetland. Unfamiliar passerines chirped from deep within tall grasses. Coots, shovelers, a few mallards, and an avocet paddled and poked through the man-made ponds. At the edge of the marsh, tractor-trailer rigs on Interstate 5 flashed through the leafless oaks like railroad cars with no end. Slamming car doors and faint laughter drifted from joggers stretching in the parking lot. I sat on a bench, eyes closed, facing the bright sun, and thought about all the birds flitting and soaring about the planet.

The godwits' annual flight to New Zealand is the longest nonstop bird journey in the world, but other migrations are just as spectacular. A young wandering albatross, hatched on a midoceanic islet, opens its eleven-foot wings and does not return to land for seven years. In Mexican towns, bird fanatics have counted ninety thousand hawks migrating overhead in a single day. Warblers, weighing as much as a coin, cross the Gulf of Mexico from Venezuela to Louisiana. Arctic terns feed beside Alaskan glaciers in July and amidst Antarctic ice in January.

For millions of years, changing climates, advancing glaciers, disappearing land bridges, and shifting food sources have pushed and honed the feat of bird migration. In addition to tracking the sun, moon, stars, and magnetic fields, birds can sense faint odors, polarized light, barometric pressure, even low-frequency sound waves bouncing halfway around the world. Birds are able to accommodate gradual changes, adjusting their migratory maps through the generations. Sudden changes are another story.

"Migratory birds," warns ornithologist Scott Weidensaul, "are facing what may be their biggest test since the earth entered the ice ages, nearly three million years ago, and maybe their biggest challenge ever. Migration depends upon links—food, safe havens, quiet roost sites, clean water, and a host of other resources, strung out in due measure and regular occurrence along routes that may cross thousands of miles. But we are breaking those links with abandon. Whereas most natural changes in climate or habitat are incremental, spread out over many hundreds, even thousands of bird generations, we are altering the landscape of migration in a heartbeat."

If my friend is right, if parenthood is about having your heart bound about beyond your control, then loving cranes is good training for a father-to-be. While I was sitting in the tiny remnant of wetlands, a familiar twitter, barely audible above the freeway din, snapped my attention. A slow scan of the blue sky revealed a single crane passing five hundred feet overhead. It was flying hard, trying to catch a wavering flock a few miles to the north. With luck, I'd hear the voice of this same bird winging over my home in two months. The crane faced days of headwinds and miles of open sky, stitching daily flights between nights roosting in ever-shrinking wetlands. I faced a half day of grumpy airport security guys and cramped airline seats.

It was quiet and snowing when I finally parked at the edge of our meadow. I shut the engine down, opened the door, and let the silence flood over me. I walked slowly along the curved path beside the creek. A raven called and I turned to see Kim strolling up behind me, all grins and mischief. "I stopped by this morning to crank up your woodstove," he said. "Should be toasty in there by now."

Kim grabbed one of my bags and walked me to the house. We kicked off our boots and I put water on for cocoa.

"So, how'd it go?" he asked. "Did you get Californicated?"

"We are all Californicated. There is no escape."

We settled in close to the stove. Halfway through the story of our cranes living in a cornfield below sea level, we were both laughing. Maybe being home made me giddy—or maybe it is truly absurd that the thirsty millions in the City of Angels draw water that is replaced by the sea that poisons the fields where the oldest bird on the planet now lives. Maybe laughter is like a thermal: a free ride to a view we can't reach on our own. Maybe humor is the only way to accept that staying still offers no escape when part of one's heart insists on moving.

Chapter Fifteen

LIFTING SHADOWS

ANYA STOOD AT THE STOVE flipping sourdough pancakes. She handed me a stack and sat down with her own plate.

"Notice anything new?" she asked, pouring maple syrup on top of melting butter. Her hair seemed the same. Her ratty nightgown just as ratty as ever.

"Uh . . . help me out."

"I'm not sick, you bozo." Anya closed her mouth around a forkful of pancake and managed to chew and smile at the same time.

"It's been three months," she added. "I think this one is going to stick around."

"You're looking a little pudgy."

"That's more than just a pancake in there," Anya said, patting her belly.

Anya suddenly grabbed my arm. "Listen!" Straining, eyes closed, I heard them too. We looked at each other and ran for the door. The meadow, just melting out from plates of dense snow, squished beneath our boots. We stood on the brown grass, heads tilted back, and spun slow circles, doing the where-are-they-dance?

"There," Anya pointed. "A couple hundred moving north."

After the dark silence of winter, the sound of cranes was like color bleeding into a black-and-white world. The cranes were high, sliding along the edge of sight. My eyes watered, straining to maintain a grip on the filament of birds; look away and they vanished into the high gray.

"They're not going to stop, are they?" Anya said.

"Nope, they got altitude, a tailwind, and a thousand miles to go," I responded.

When the cranes finally disappeared, Anya and I still stood in our meadow, arms around each other, searching for following flocks. None came. Finally, with Anya shivering in her nightgown, we went back inside.

After breakfast, Anya sorted through the piles of hand-me-down clothes crowding the floor of our tiny home. Within days of sharing the news of Anya's pregnancy, the boxes started to arrive, filled with cloth diapers and flannel pajamas, striped shirts and flowered hats, rubber boots and plastic sandals—gifts from sisters, aunts, and grandparents. While Anya organized outfits, I built shelves in the few spots not already jumbled with our own stuff. As soon as I got a board nailed in place, Anya covered it with a stack of folded clothes.

Except in sleep, I have never known Anya's body to be still. From the moment she awakes, she casts about for ways to care for others. Mixing waffle batter, she'll work down the phone list looking for a neighbor in need of breakfast. After scooping the snow from our path, she'll carry her shovel to someone else's driveway. Like the Dog of God's dedication to Bolivian children, Anya devotes her full attention to each patient entering her exam room. When a meeting or lecture forces her to sit still, Anya's fingers busy themselves with the rhythmic click of knitting needles. Her passion for berry picking is fueled by the vision of pies and jams she'll later share with family and friends.

But no number of waffles, cleared driveways, patched-up patients, warm sweaters, or hot pies could produce the glow of satisfaction emanating from Anya's pregnant body. Bundling tiny socks, folding miniature pants, and keeping a growing lump of cells warm filled her with a depth of contentment I'd never seen.

"When everything is moving in the same direction and at the same speed," wrote the French philosopher Blaise Pascal, "nothing seems to be moving, as aboard a ship. When all are moving precipitously toward excesses, none seems to be so moving. He who stops makes the mad rush of the others perceptible, as would a fixed point."

Pregnancy did not slow Anya. If anything, the chores of nest build-ing extended her to-do list. But the task of creating new life was effort-less. With every cell of her being in service Anya was, for the first time, freed from the drive to do more. Even in sleep she could now take care of someone else. Her serenity was like a still stone in the mad rush of my own mind.

———

Where Anya was held in place by love, I was pushed by fear and prodded by anger, mad at a culture willing to trade beauty for profit. In an effort to keep the Arctic quiet and free of industry, I bustled through the bark and scurry of airports. In hopes of keeping the sky filled with cranes, the hillsides covered in trees, the streams thick with fish, the atmosphere free of toxins, I responded to every action alert that came through my mail-box. I dialed my senators, wrote my congressman, and made my dona-tions. I volunteered as president of the local conservation group. I served on the board of the regional conservation council. I worked as the direc-tor of the local land trust.

But living with a woman calmly making life made my efforts to protect the planet feel frantic and diffuse. The few months before our child emerged from the sheltering warmth of Anya's body was not enough time to change the world. No matter how many phone calls I made or road trips I took, no matter how many meetings I attended or donations I made, I could not stop the news of war from bleeding into our home, could not prevent the trickle of atmospheric mercury from finding its way into our rain barrel, could not insure the cranes would always come.

―――――

New shelves filled, baby paraphernalia still cluttered the floor. I began pulling books to make more room. The unused volumes carried years of dust. Others bore the smudge of finger grease and stains of coffee spills. The dusty stories I placed in a box bound for the second-hand store. Among the dog-eared books reclaiming their spot on the shelf were such titles as *Losing Ground, The End of Nature, The Long Emergency,* and *Collapse.* The authors, like me, are driven to reverse our culture's damage to the earth. But what happens when the pace and scale of damage outstrips our ability to restore and repair? What happens when we get caught up in the mad rush to catch something beyond our reach?

While removing David James Duncan's *My Story as Told by Water* from the shelf, the book fell open to this underlined sentence: "When your heart's home is being annihilated, your peace and serenity are in deep shit and that's all there is to it." Scott Russell Sanders's *Hunting for Hope* fell open to these highlighted words: "In order to live in hope we needn't believe that everything will turn out well. We need only believe we are on the right track."

In the following months, as our child stretched and pushed the skin of Anya's belly, I started to admit I was both in deep shit and on the wrong track. If, at the end of the day (or pregnancy), nothing had really changed, then why all the work? What is the cost of getting caught up in the mad rush? What do I not see while focused on a failed future?

Once again, Anya was the calm answer to my questions. Now that her body was shared property she had started taking great care of it. She decreased her hours at work. She bought organic vegetables, refused pesticide-laden fruits. She gave up beer, ate vitamins by the fistful, and got plenty of sleep. She read every article she could find on nutrition and stocked our pantry with whole grains and fibers. She did for her child what she'd never done for herself.

Aside from one very determined little cell, our child had no direct connection to my body. Since leaving Lindy's lab, I had been left with no obvious role in the pregnancy. Fatherhood was a growing but nonetheless invisible abstraction. I continued to pull cold beer from the creek. I could eat hormone-rich bacon and pesticide-painted strawberries all day long with no ill effect on our fetus. But I'd been around children enough to know they are sponges, soaking up the anger or joy, the anxiety or seren-ity of the people around them. Anya's wholesome food made me realize I'd been feeding myself a steady diet of discouragement and despair.

Whether working on behalf of Bolivian orphans or Alaskan cranes, I have been motivated, like so many people, by what Scott Sanders calls the "bite of conscience." The sharp teeth feed the impulse to answer all cries for help. But what happens when the cries swell beyond our ability to respond? How do we keep from being buried by a swelling sense of failure?

Children are born unburdened by guilt, their malleable brains unscarred by the jaws of conscience. Anticipating our child's joy made me aware of my lack of it, made me aware I had accepted despondency and discouragement as inevitable, even proper, responses to news of war and loss. Just as my father shed tears on a quiet hillside, I braced against the diminution of beauty breaking my child's heart. Yet I knew I did not want to stain my baby with the loss of things not yet loved. I would not burden a child with fixing what they did not break.

So I gave it all up. I stepped away from the presidency of the local watchdog group. I resigned from the board of the regional conservation council. I let the action alerts pile up unanswered. I declined invitations for more road trips. Not only was I fighting a battle I could not win, but I was losing a battle I did not want to fight. If I could not ensure a peaceful, intact world, what then could I offer our child?

There were no cries for help coming from the life in Anya's belly. It just did its thing: growing bigger every day with the confidence of tides, the faith of cranes. Watching the joy swell within Anya, I began to question my professor's conviction that beauty was diminishing. Sure there are ugly things in the world, but who can really believe beauty is finite and shrinking while watching a fresh being squirm within your lover's belly? While Anya provided our child the nourishing warmth of own her body, I vowed to uncover the nourishing expanse of my own joy.

Chapter Sixteen

SUCK IT ALL IN

GREEN FINGERS OF NORTHERN LIGHTS flickered over the mountaintops as we drove to the Juneau hospital. A white sliver of moon hung in the southern sky. I pulled over and shut off the headlights to watch the show. Anya grimaced and placed her hand on her belly. "Better keep moving," she said.

Hours later the contractions gathered strength. Anya sang her way through the pain—no words, just a sustained clear tone. I sang with her. Our music filled the maternity ward. The staff monitored Anya's progress without leaving the nursing station.

After two sleepless days and forty hours of body-wracking pain the caesarean crew was called in. My vision of a magical birth never involved the bright lights and busy technology of the operating room. But when that blood-smeared baby was lifted from Anya's belly and handed to me, disappointment was overshadowed by relief. Someone handed me a pair of scissors and I snipped through the tough, twisted cord. The moment our daughter cut loose with a high, sharp squall, my desires became meaningless. I was just happy to have a healthy child; happy to have Anya safe and healthy and in the hands of professionals who knew how to repair the open mess of her body.

That night Anya slept through her exhaustion while I held our daughter in a rocking chair. Resting lightly in my arms, she felt as delicate as a hummingbird. I rocked for hours, watching her sleeping face, dozing myself, waking, surprised she was still there. In the wee hours, I called family and friends to announce the arrival of Linnea Rain.

Later that morning, holding Linnea Rain, I headed for the door but was stopped by a nurse who explained that, for security reasons, babies could not leave the premises until discharged. I nodded and smiled, then slipped out when the nurse checked in on another patient. I climbed the forested hill behind the hospital, hiking until my legs burned and my heart pounded. When I could no longer hear slamming doors and whining wheels I crouched in the wet moss and leaned against the rough bark of a hemlock tree. Linnea Rain lay in my arms like an oversized burrito. I flipped back the blanket and exposed her tiny face. She wrinkled her nose when a drop of cold rain splashed her cheek. Another drop hit her forehead, a rain forest baptism. She squirmed but did not wake up.

A newborn is life trusting itself. For a baby, faith is no more a choice than gravity. My daughter knew, without question, that she would be cared for—kept warm, fed, held, loved. Sitting in the quiet woods, holding eight pounds of faith, I suddenly felt the freedom of Anya's clarity of purpose, her devotion to others. I felt the joy of knowing our child was right to trust, that betrayal was not an option. I cried there in the woods; tears of gratitude that she was here, in my arms, breathing, confident in my care; tears of humility that I should be blessed with such a gift; tears of relief that the wild ride of labor was over. And gratitude again for the chance to share the place I love.

Back in the hospital, the nurse scowled at my rain-dampened hair and Linnea's water-splotched blanket. I smiled and walked on by. A raven croaked when I opened the door to Anya's room. Kim and his wife, Melanie, had just flown in from Gustavus, eager to meet their new neighbor. Kim laughed when he held Linnea; Melanie cried. When Mary

Cook stopped by, she cradled the baby and settled onto the hospital bed like she'd never move again. Cards and flowers crowded the recovery room. People called to hear the story of Linnea's birth—such a big fan club for such a little person.

Anya healed fast. After two nights in the hospital, we moved to Anya's childhood home on Lena Cove. We placed the placenta on the beach for the birds. Magpies showed up first, pecking at the tough membrane. Soon a pair of ravens swooped down for the feast. I held Linnea to the window but she slept through the whole show.

When Anya had the strength to travel, we flew home to Gustavus and began packing for Lemesurier Island. We boated across Icy Strait on a calm day in early December. Bob met our boat at the creek bank. Anya handed the bundled baby over the bow. Bob smiled, said nothing. He carried the precious load across the yard, welcoming his new acquaintance to the island.

Linnea was just a few weeks old when we arrived and still had the scrawny look of a newborn. During the next month, she grew like bread dough with too much yeast. Her belly soon hung over her diaper, her thighs swelled into puffy rolls, and her wrist creases collected lint.

———

In the years since Frank's death, Anya had developed a sit-and-wait style of hunting. While I prowled an entire hillside, Anya would hunker down in a small pocket of muskeg or sit in an open stretch of forest. When deer appeared, Anya often let them pass. Holding out for the steady sure shots, she has never missed.

But now, with a newborn to carry, Anya had no interest in her rifle. With a gorgeous creature in her arms, she had no need to look for one in the woods. I pulled my hunting gear together while Anya strapped Linnea to her chest and struggled to zip her coat over the load.

"Here, take mine," I offered, pulling my down jacket from my pack.
"You don't need it?"

"Not as much as you two do."

Bundled in my oversized coat, my girls headed out for a hike on the sunlit beach. I shouldered my rifle and slipped into the forest shade.

Throughout the years we've placed the heads and hides of all our deer between the arcing roots of two large spruces not far from the house. I chose the spot because it was easy to imagine a deer waiting out a storm curled in the moss-draped bowl of roots. A few months earlier, before heading to Juneau for the birth, Anya and I had laid the remains of two deer atop the pile of bones. I now walked the familiar trail from the house to find those hides twisted together, white undersides turned and exposed by the scraping and pecking of ravens and eagles. During her last weeks of pregnancy, Anya had eaten the muscles that had once filled those skins, molecules winding through her body, twisting through the umbilical cord, and adding their weight to the growing lump of cells we now call Linnea Rain.

Standing in the woods, breathing the subtle odor of rotting flesh, I had to close my eyes and concentrate in order to pull back an image of the deers' beauty: delicate whiskers off the chin, long sweeping eyelashes, curved funnel ears, black convolutions of nose. I opened my eyes to tufts of hair lying in a hatched pattern round the rumpled skins. The skulls were worked clean, the bones pierced, the brains eaten. The only flesh remaining was the rough, ridged lining of the roof of the mouth and bits of gray gums around the teeth. One of the lower jaws was pulled free of the skull and lay ten feet away. The jaw on the other skull was attached but pried wide in a still and tongueless grin.

I left the bones and climbed deeper into the valley. An hour later, while I was thinking about my girls on the beach, a snort and flash of brown snapped my attention. The deer was close, had likely listened to my approach for long minutes before running off. This is typical for me. I often blunder into several deer, watch them bound away, before finally gathering enough concentration to push the daydreams aside.

In the widely spaced trees on the valley floor I forced myself to slow down: two, maybe three steps, then a minute or more scanning for a flicker of life. I was holding still when a deer stepped from behind a tree not fifty yards away. I slowly raised my binoculars and studied the stubby-faced fawn. The young deer was oblivious to my presence. I searched the surrounding forest and eventually found its mother standing behind a clump of devil's club, alert and motionless, staring at me.

This late in the year, the fawn was old enough to survive on its own. Although it is legal to shoot does and this one was close, I didn't raise my rifle. With my own child held close to her mother's chest, I had no stomach for the thought of orphans. The doe and I continued to stare while the fawn nibbled plants near the base of a tree. I remained frozen until my legs started to twitch and ache. When I knelt to relieve knotting muscles, the movement confirmed the deer's suspicion and, with a nervous twitch of her tail, she stepped onto a path cutting steeply uphill.

She followed the trail for a moment and stopped. Only then did I notice the buck. He'd been there all along, staring down beneath the wide spread of antlers. I slowly swung the rifle into place, released the safety, and centered the buck's head in the scope's circle. I held my breath, squeezed the trigger; the forest filled with a sharp avalanche of sound. The buck's belly flashed white as he tumbled downhill. The doe gathered four legs into a single great spring and bounded uphill, followed closely by her fawn.

I stepped slowly to the deer: a buck in its prime—four, maybe five years old, neck still thick from the recent rut, every hair immaculate, antlers graceful, hooves delicate, body still twitching with life. I dropped my pack and rifle and left the deer. I sat in the still woods to let my nerves settle.

When I returned the deer was still. I drew my knife through the thick winter fur and opened the belly. Entrails and stomach bulged through the slit. I reached deep into the warm body to cut through the trachea, then pulled the steaming pile of organs onto the moss. I cut the heart and liver free and placed them in a plastic bag. When I knelt to wash my hands in a nearby stream, the icy water swirled briefly red, then flashed clear.

In the following days, we processed the deer into jerky, liver pâté, and burger. We had fried sausage for breakfast, broiled steaks for dinner, leftovers for lunch. Anya's appetite swelled beyond my own. "This girl is going to suck me dry," Anya said, snacking on a slice of backstrap. "Wonder how much this little milk monkey weighs?"

Bob pulled a twenty-pound sack of flour off the shelf. Flour in one hand, Linnea balanced in the other, he guessed her weight to be around sixteen pounds.

"About double her birth weight," I replied

Anya settled on the couch and lifted her shirt to give Linnea one of her many midday meals. Linnea kicked her pudgy legs as she nursed. I listened to her gurgled slurping and thought about rain and blueberry bushes, sun and skunk cabbage, dirt and hemlock needles all flowing through the deer out Anya's swollen breast and finding a place in the fat rolls on our child's thighs.

"She'll never be more a part of this island than she is right now," I said.

"Damn near pure Lemesurier," Bob agreed.

A few days before Christmas, Bob packed up to spend the holidays with family in Seattle. I helped load his gear into the boat. We stood on the shore, each resting a hand on the boat's gunwale.

"I'm not sure if having you on the island makes it easier or harder to leave," Bob said.

"Leaving family to visit family hardly makes sense," I replied.

"It will make it easier to come back," Bob said as he jumped aboard. "Push me off, Hankster."

Swirling snow squalls greeted us Christmas morning. Anya and I munched through an entire pan of cinnamon rolls while Linnea grunted and wheezed in her bed near the woodstove. Blue sky and sun split open the afternoon. We bundled the baby in sweaters and set off in the bright sun. The curved cut of deer hooves marked the snow-covered trail in front of us.

Late afternoon we reached the shore of the frozen lake in the island's center. Sunbeams slid sharply through the trees. Anya settled against a trunk to give her daughter a snack. As Linnea nursed, I spotted a doe and fawn crossing the hillside above us. I pointed and Anya turned to look. The deer stopped and stared back. Linnea made smacking noises, sucking it all in.

Chapter Seventeen

LINOLEUM DOUGHNUT

SUNNY MORNING IN LATE APRIL, Anya made coffee while I spoon-fed Linnea mushed carrots. I heard them first. With a whoop I yanked my daughter from her high chair and ran for the meadow. Anya chased after us, bathrobe wrapped over her ragged nightgown, coffee cup in hand. I held Linnea above my head to get her closer to the wheeling cranes. She wrapped sticky fingers into my hair and shrieked with delight, orange goo spread across her face. She didn't look up, never focused on the birds; her glee was a response to her parents' joy.

She was almost a year old when the cranes returned in the fall. I dug potatoes while Linnea sat in the mud, combing chubby fingers through the dirt. "Look! Up there above the trees," I said, pointing. She glanced briefly skyward and then turned back to the worm wiggling in her filthy fist. The cacophonous chorus of a thousand cranes could not distract her from the life in her hands.

It's boggling the terrain she covered in the time it took the cranes to make the next round trip; from baby babble to singing "Puff the Magic Dragon," from clutching at a mobile to throwing rocks in the sea, from suckling a nipple to stuffing deer heart in her mouth with her own greasy fingers. At first anything flying was simply a "biwd." But quickly she teased out the loud honk of geese from the high twitter of eagles, the raspy croak of ravens from the lisp of chickadees.

During her first fall migration, Linnea was a diapered mud-ball. Twelve months later, she toddled about, tossing dirt-caked spuds into the bucket of wash water with a satisfying splash. When the first crane called from beyond the horizon, I didn't say anything; I just leaned on my shovel and watched my girl. When the birds passed overhead, Linnea pointed her pudgy fingers skyward and shouted, "Look, Papa! Cranes!"

Linnea was almost four when I removed the training wheels from her bike. I jogged along as she wobbled up and down the dirt road, tires crunching through the fallen cottonwood leaves. All evening small flocks of cranes drifted in, wings set for the wetlands. Linnea giggled nervously, teetering on the edge of control. I hooted sounds of encouragement, breathless from running. Wave after wave of cranes called out, tired from a long day's flight. After parking her bike, Linnea unsnapped her helmet and took my hand. We lingered outside the house, watching the sun drop through the trees and listening to the distant whisper of cranes.

A few months later the cranes were settled into the California corn-fields and our meadow was silent and frozen. Sunrise saturated the tree-tops with an orange glow. The house was chilly. It was time to get up and light a fire but I lingered in the warmth of our bed. Linnea lay curled in my arms staring out the bedside window. "Papa, the world is beautiful. All the animals are beautiful. Nature only made one mistake."

"What's that, sweetie?"

"It made us."

"Why do you say that?"

"Because we do things that we know are bad for the earth."

"Like what?"

"Oh, you know, like drive cars and buy things we don't need."

I tried to dissuade her. I told her we are just as beautiful as the trees, the deer, the cranes, the sky. But she shook her head, convinced she was a living mistake.

———

A young crane on its first migration and a fetus twisting in its warm womb are both bound by an allegiance they are powerless to break. Only after the umbilical cord is snipped does the vast circuitry of the mind begin to invent stories of isolation and separateness. I have lived within walls of guilt for the privilege of being born into affluence while children around the world go hungry. I've swallowed the bitterness of anger toward those I blame for destroying what I love. I've shouldered the burden of righteousness, believing in my own choices while scorning others. I've struggled through the darkness of loss, the relentless spread of asphalt. And through it all I have been living in the same world that cranes have been flying through for millions of years. The same world Linnea came into with such fearless grace.

In her six short years, Linnea has been surrounded by critters and creeks. She has pulled the hide off deer and held the still-beating heart of salmon. She has followed her mother through acre after acre of berry patches and washed hundreds of pounds of garden spuds. She's a happy child; our home is filled with laughter and music, our family steeped in gratitude. Still, at times Linnea feels we are an ugly species. She repeats it at odd moments: out playing in the snow, getting pulled in the sled, looking through the skylight at the stars just before sleep.

Each time the words sting, a sharp reminder that she's absorbed the very thing I did not want to pass on. Disdain for our own species is, like racism, a prejudice that must be learned. I wish I could blame someone else, but Linnea has never watched television. She is too young to log on to the computer. I rarely turn on the radio, unwilling to fill her head with the endless stories of suicide bombings and political scandals. Along with Anya, I am, for now, her closest teacher. Just because she is playing with dolls does not mean she isn't listening to my phone calls and our dinner conversations. She quietly soaks up my frustration with politicians unwilling to deal with shrinking icecaps; she picks up my dismay with a country willing to kill for oil; she senses my sadness over the convergence of congestion and cranes.

Last year Linnea's preschool teacher asked each student what they planned to do when they grew up. The teacher printed the responses on a black picture frame bordering the face of each graduate. The framed photos were presented at an end-of-the-year ceremony filled with skits, songs, Kool-Aid, and cake with too-sweet frosting. Linnea's words, surrounding her broad smile, now hang on our living room wall: *When I grow up I will take care of the earth with my cousin Jakob.*

Fatherhood has been a steady lesson in patience, an endless tutorial in the art of enough. I'll pack snacks for a long hike only to spend the afternoon on my knees helping Linnea crush up spruce cones, dissect flowers, and poke fingers into the grass nests of voles. We'll explore for hours before unpacking our picnic of apple slices and cheese chunks within sight of the house. With Linnea's small hand wrapped on my large finger, I am constantly pulled from a fretful future into the marvelous present.

I am, of course, proud of my daughter's preschool ambitions. But I also cringe to feel the bite of conscience sink its teeth at such a tender age. I worry that Linnea and I are trading places; as she blesses me with a curiosity tied to the present, I burden her with a responsibility locked in the future.

My own education failed to provide the tools to dig my way through the cold statistics of exponential growth on a finite planet. My professors convinced me the world's beauty was diminishing without offering guidance through the subsequent despair. No one told me that the fear of loss is, itself, the stealthiest of thieves.

———

I've always been a sucker for doom. I bought into the whole Y2K thing. It didn't take much to get ready. With our garden, root cellar, and wood-stove, Anya and I were pretty well prepared for a technological train wreck. I did buy extra blades for my bow saw in anticipation of the town's one gas pump fritzing out and my chainsaw running dry. I also picked up several cases of canning jar lids so we could preserve salmon and venison when the electricity quit flowing to our freezer. I even stocked up on ammo. Not a lot of bullets, just enough to kill a few deer a year for the rest of my life, provided I didn't miss much.

Prepared and confident, Anya and I opted to start the new century at a wilderness hot springs. The first of January found us soaking with Kim and Melanie in the beachside tub. We floated around, trying to imagine the chaos of traffic and commerce grinding to a standstill around the globe.

"Tide is still working," said Kim, gazing at the kelp-draped rocks.

"Yep, water is still hot too. How bad could it be?"

A few days later, when a boat came to pick us up, we eagerly gathered as the captain nosed into the beach.

"Well?"

"Nothing," he said. "Not a damn thing."

I was both embarrassed and, I have to admit, disappointed. No catas-trophe, not even a failed traffic light. I thought (hoped) Y2K would be the perfect wake-up call; a tiny oversight rumbling into an avalanche to shake us from our enchantment with technology. In my fantasy, people would emerge from stalled cars and grounded planes, from behind dead espresso machines and jammed cash registers with a shared sense of vul-nerability. People around the globe would see the frailty inherent in ship-ping grain and apples across oceans. They'd buy hoes, find vacant lots, and become farmers. The perfect glitch; our last chance to embrace the earth's cycles before we knocked those cycles totally out of whack. I was frustrated to see the unsustainable once again sustained.

Like most of the nearly seven billion people on the planet, I have not read the reports from the intergovernmental panel on climate change. I rely, instead, on much smarter minds to sort through the volumes of graphs and columns of data. In the introduction to *Down to the Wire: Confronting Climate Collapse,* David Orr promises to be as "optimistic as a careful reading of the evidence permits." A mere twenty pages later Orr writes, "Some may quibble about the timing, but it is clear that we are headed toward a global disaster that has the potential to destroy civilization."

When I bought bullets and saw blades for Y2K, I was not yet a father. I was thinking about taking care of myself, my wife, and a few immediate neighbors. I just needed Lemesurier and a few other places to stay wild for my remaining years. Parenthood messed everything up. My plans of isolation did not account for the wanderlust that may carry my child far from home. My imaginary bubble was not big enough to accommodate the breadth of Linnea's days.

I, of course, want every autumn of my daughter's life filled with chortling cranes. I want her to hear the rich harmonies of wolves when she steps out to pee. But should Linnea find herself living in a city, should those cranes and wolves be silenced, I want my daughter to not lose sight of all the beauty that remains, most importantly her own. Of course I cannot teach what I have not learned. And what I want to learn is how to live a life like Miriam, a woman I knew for a week years ago.

Miriam lived in the Alzheimer's wing of a retirement home in Grand Rapids, Michigan. Crafty engineers designed the facility in a giant circle so the residents could shuffle in an endless loop in constant sight of the nurse's station. Most all of us are familiar with the sights and sounds of such places: the withered bodies, the wrinkled faces, the sterile smell, the endless cries for help from an open door, the nursing staff cheerfully accustomed to such cries. The real terror of these places lies not in the hazed minds of the residents but in the vivid fears of the visitor. To think this could be our fate: years spent ambling around a linoleum doughnut not knowing we are not going anywhere.

I was led to this particular doughnut by Anya's grandfather, Sherman Lepard. He brought us along to check in on his lifelong friend and neighbor. At ninety-three, Sherm was mostly deaf and blind. Perhaps that is why he seemed unperturbed by the scuffling corpses and delirious pleas for help. Or maybe the frequency of his visits made him, like the nurses, comfortable with the scene. In either case, Sherm moved round the corridor with a quick, confident step. He rapped his knuckles on a door and opened it without waiting for an answer. We entered a small room pleasantly decorated with paintings and knickknacks. Tall windows looked out on pruned shrubs and clipped lawn. Sherm brusquely shook the lump curled beneath a colorfully crocheted blanket.

"Miriam, wake up!" he barked. "It's me, Sherm." Miriam slowly pushed herself to sitting, gray hair all askew. She passed a blank look over our three faces, then settled her gaze on a painting.

"Oh my, that is beautiful!" she exclaimed. Her eyes darted to the flicker of birds grabbing seeds just beyond her window. "Oh my, aren't they beautiful." She looked me straight in the eyes and asked, "Do you know this tune?" Without waiting for a reply, she closed her eyes, lifted her soft voice into song, "Lighthouse light, keep on shining. Keep those ships . . . "

"Miriam, this is my granddaughter, Anya," Sherm interrupted. "She's a doctor."

"My, that's a lovely painting. Say, do you know this song? Lighthouse light, keep on shining . . . This is such a lovely place to live. Do you live here?"

"My granddaughter is from Alaska," Sherm shouted.

Miriam looked at her old neighbor, blinked her eyes a few times, then proclaimed, "You should see if you can get a room here. Do you know this song? Lighthouse light, keep on shining, keep those ships from your shore . . . You know the people here are so nice."

I came back to visit Miriam each day of our weeklong visit. Each time it was the same. Miriam spent every waking breath on the verge of rapture, enchanted by a sunbeam, the flight of a bird, a melody, a painting she'd owned for years. Forgetfulness made everything fresh. There was no lost past, no worrisome future. I might not have returned to her room if I didn't have to negotiate the doughnut of terror to get there. The anxiety of her neighbors deepened my encounters with her joy. The spooked faces and pleading calls in the curved hallway made me uneasy. Miriam made me curious. What had she done with her youth? How do you live a life so that joy remains when all else fades?

Chapter Eighteen

BONES

SANDHILL CRANES DID NOT OUTLIVE DINOSAURS by being finicky. Drifting into the ice-gripped Arctic in early spring, they probe the edge of receding snow, gobbling whatever they can find: insects, grubs, spiders, arthropods, and the roots of grasses, sedges, and willows. To feed their ravenous chicks, the parents turn carnivorous. Like a robin searching for worms, they cock their heads to watch for the scurry of lemmings; they steal eggs from neighboring snow geese or peck apart baby ptarmigan to stuff down the gullets of the growing colts.

While specialized species come and go, sandhills are the masters of making do. On their winter range they pick at worms, frogs, and mice slithering and crawling across the corn and rice fields. Like coyotes and deer slipping through city streets, these birds skirt the brink of extinction, always poking the world's changing edges for someplace new to nest, something new to eat.

We too are adapting. As a boy, my grandfather could not imagine the interstates and moon landings, the Holocaust and Hiroshima. Likewise, it is impossible to predict the events that will transform the century of my daughter's life. It's safe to assume the pace of change will accelerate, that the world outside Linnea's crib will have little resemblance to the world beyond her deathbed. It is wise to consider the words Thomas Berry penned after a lifetime of reflection: "It is already determined that our children and grandchildren will live amid the ruined infrastructures of the industrial world and amid the ruin of the natural world itself." In such a world we cannot afford to be finicky in feeding our appetite for beauty. In such a world there is no room for the illusion that we are ugly, that we do not belong.

Nowhere am I more aware of my own beauty than gathered around the growing pile of bones on Lemesurier Island. Over twenty years have passed since my gun refused to fire and I watched the jawless doe walk away from me in the frigid forest. Since then I have never been sure what I will feel in the moments after pulling the trigger. When I make a poor shot and the deer suffers, I feel reproachful for my impatience. When the shot is well placed and the animal drops in its tracks I feel a mix of exhilaration and gratitude. Regardless of my marksmanship, I often feel the sting of regret. I'll walk to a dying animal and want to reverse the damage; to replace the bulged out eye and tighten the shattered skull. It is still baffling that I can, with a twitch of a finger, end the life of such an exquisitely gentle being.

Each year family and friends gather with the intent to give thanks to the deer and make sense of the violence. A ritual has grown around the bones. I must admit that the pipe, the singing, the stuffing of plants into a dead animal's mouth feels, at times, hokey and contrived. But each fall, when the stories of our lives, the ones we always carry but seldom share, tumble out around the bones, I am reminded of the need for ceremony.

A few years back, Dad helped carry the remains through the woods. We arranged them atop the older bones. We sat in the rain and talked for over an hour. We were just about to head back to the cabin when Dad began the story of Grandpa's last day. What he ate. What he said. He described the weight of his father dying in his arms. How hard it would have been not to be there. The deer coaxed that story from my dad; I would never have heard it had we not chosen to stand so close to the deer.

Linnea slept through her first visit to the graveyard. It was the day after Christmas, the forest covered in an inch of dry, fine-grained snow. Anya shrugged into my oversized coat and zipped Linnea into its warm folds. I tucked the deer's head, hide, and feet onto a blue plastic sled. The load slid easily on the fresh snow. The rumpled skins and rotting smell from earlier deer were veiled beneath frozen crystals. Anya lifted her clear voice as I spread the hide.

Deer before us
Deer behind us
Deer under our feet

I gathered bunchberry leaves, pushed them between the buck's cold lips and joined the chant.

Deer within us
Deer over us
Let all around us be deer

We cycled round and round, our voices an octave apart, our child nestled against Anya's reverberating chest. We kept singing as I slipped the curved antler pipe from its leather pouch. Linnea squirmed in her sleep, kicking the coat just as she used to bulge Anya's skin.

Never had the words of our little song felt so true. Nothing on the island—the deer, the snow, my daughter, even I—was any more or less beautiful than anything else. Sitting across that flat stretch of skin from Anya, I no longer struggled with the power of a piece of lead zipping through the forest with bone-shattering, lung-tearing precision. Alongside those bones, I knew that nothing really dies. I knew I was every bit as beautiful as the deer. The violence of the hunt, like the pain and blood of birth, simply marks the shifting of forms.

We stopped singing and I reached for a pinch of dried leaves. Gratitude pushed aside all feelings of regret and guilt, all thought of judgment and fear. I whispered thanks for the gifts of deer and child. I tucked the leaves into the antler's blackened bowl and passed Anya the pipe. She took a pinch of leaves and said, "I wish you could meet her, Daddy. She is beautiful. She'll climb your mountain someday." I held a lighter while Anya sucked the little flame into our prayers. The hushed crackle of burning leaves, a tendril of smoke disappearing into the forest.

That was six years ago. Linnea now leads the way to the graveyard. Last fall we followed her down the familiar trail, watching her duck under the leafless stalks of devil's club and swing her short legs over downed logs. She carried the lower ends of two furred legs and my buckskin pouch. She cradled the load like firewood, mittened hands curving up and back toward her face. The hooves were shiny with rain, as black as the tufts of hair poking from her wool hat. Anya carried the other two legs. My arms wrapped around the bulky roll of hide still attached to the antlered head.

High overhead branches thrashed and whistled in the full force of a southwest storm. Crossing the open yard from the Ibachs' old house, we tucked our chins and hunched our shoulders against the driving sleet. The forest floor was littered with twigs torn free by the gale. Linnea stopped near the wide scatter of bones. She slowly scanned the scene, finding more antlers and overturned skulls the longer she looked. Some were barely visible, obscured by tendrils of moss. The skulls from last year's hunt were on the surface, picked to a clean white by the hungry beaks of ravens.

I faced the deer's head east, toward the sunrise, and spread the hide on top of the other bones. I took the legs from my daughter, two more from her mother, and tucked them under the circle of fur. Linnea placed the buckskin bundle on the deer's back. She pulled off her mittens and walked to the base of a tree. She returned with a fistful of dogwood leaves. She lifted the deer's stiff lip with a thumb and poked the waxy leaves into the lifeless mouth with the fingers of her other hand. We spread raincoats on the wet ground and sat. Linnea leaned forward and unwound the cord binding the leather pouch. As she opened the bundle she began to sing. Anya and I glanced at each other, smiled, and joined in.

———

I don't want to be cremated. I want my whole body buried. No casket or clothes. Just cold skin against the wet earth. I want the grave to be shallow. I want roots of small plants to bite into my thigh, wrap tiny living threads around dying bone. I want to be pulled back into daylight and spun back through the deer. I'm sure I'd be less poetic about the whole deal if someone or something else was carrying the gun trying to turn me into a stir-fry. But every time I try to peer around the backside of death, I find life staring back at me.

Above us the tree tips whip in the ongoing storm. Around the pile of bones, the protective trunks of spruce and hemlock buffer the gusts to an easy breeze. I hold the pipe and feel those tall trees sheltering us from so much more than wind. On the island we are insulated from poverty and pollution, crime and injustice. Bathed in the rainforest's beauty, it is blessedly easy to let the torrent of bad news fade to the edge of awareness.

Days on the island will likely diminish as Linnea is pulled into the vortex of school and friends. A few years from now hunting trips will get squeezed between volleyball tournaments and algebra tests. Already, time around these bones accounts for a fraction of our year. Soon Anya and I will walk the familiar trail without our girl. Like Frank did for Anya, I will seal each hunt into a letter and send it along to wherever Linnea ends up.

Reaching for a pinch of dried leaves, I pray that the precious few days on the island are enough, that the gratitude gathered round these bones will follow my daughter wherever she goes. Before passing the pipe, I add, "May you always know your beauty, Linnea. If you ever lose sight of it, may you again find it here."

Anya spoke of seeing herself alongside Frank when she looks at Linnea in the woods. "I am thankful to know where we all come from and where we go," Anya said, tucking leaves into the blackened bowl. Linnea held the pipe for long minutes, her eyes focused on a far-off place. She stuffed in a pinch of leaves and passed the pipe back to me without a word.

High overhead the storm hummed through the treetops, rising to a high whine with each pulse of wind. Hanging from low branches, strands of pale green lichen lifted and swayed in the breeze. Smoke curled and eddied quickly away. I tucked the antler pipe, still warm, back into its soft leather pouch. Anya stood and rubbed her cold stiffened legs. "I've got to get moving," she said, "I'm about frozen."

Linnea kneeled and whispered something to the deer. I couldn't make out the words. She took her mother's hand and together they trudged down the trail. I lingered for a moment, staring at the buck, bunchberry leaves poking from his lips. Moss will bury his bones. Time will cloud my memory. The deer, for a time, will walk on two legs, ride a bike, learn to read, and pick out a few new tunes on the fiddle.

I whispered a final thanks, then turned to catch up with my girls. Stepping from the sheltering woods, we hunched our shoulders against the full fury of the storm. With squinted eyes and tilted heads we walked into the bullets of sleet shooting sideways across the yard. Waves tumbled up the creek mouth, bright white on deep green. I passed a worried look at our boat. It was still there, straining at anchor, teetering over each crest, slapping hard into the troughs.

"I'm going in for cocoa," Anya said. "Anybody coming with me?"

"Not me," Linnea answered. "I want to watch the waves. Come on, Papa."

Linnea took my hand and tugged me toward the sea. As we passed Muz and Joe's grave, I wondered how many storms blew through their forty years on the island. Did Joe leave his boat on anchor or drag it above the tide? What kind of hot drink did Muz make to replenish the heat sucked away by the wind? Why didn't they have kids? Would they have stayed on the island if they did?

The tide was huge, waves lapping higher on to the lawn than I have ever seen.

"Ouch!" Linnea shouted. "That hail hurts."

"Put your back into it," I yelled.

With waves lapping around our ankles, we lean into the storm, resting on a buffeting mattress of wind. The island, all her deer, her twin dome mountains were hidden behind the whizzing wall of snow. Smoke from the chimney whipped and eddied in a tight downdraft behind the house. Anya stood in the window, both hands around a steaming mug, watching.

"You ready for cocoa yet?" I asked, but the wind stole my words.

"What?" Linnea yelled. I leaned down and hollered alongside her hooded head. "Are you ready to go inside?"

"Not yet. Let's stay out and play."

Chapter Nineteen

SEEDS

BENEATH MOON OR SUN, STORM OR CALM, in every moment of every day for over ten million years, the voice of a sandhill crane has called out somewhere on the planet in a seamless lineage of sound. There is cohesion in the chaotic calls of cranes, an invisible thread binding living beads, stitching the flocks, tying each generation to the next.

Cranes talk to their egg-bound chicks with murmurs and clicks. The chicks imprint on the sound; they yearn to follow that voice even before breaking free of the shell. The birds grow, add their high peeps to the throaty calls of the larger flock and are soon clucking to their own offspring. Our lives too are embedded in a rich sea of sounds. While still in the womb, a fetus listens and responds to the muted tones of the world it will soon enter.

The rich diversity of sound—music and wind, laughter and bird song, sobs and sea surf, poems and snowfall, stories and crane calls—guides us through our lives and hold us in place as surely as gravity keeps our feet pinned to the spinning earth. In the absence of sound and story, prisoners, locked in solitary confinement, lose all orientation and quickly tumble toward insanity. The lineage of voices that hold us in place come from near and far, the furred and feathered, the newly born and the long dead.

Whenever I feel buried beneath the growing heap of stark statistics about rising seas and growing violence, widening ozone holes and spreading poverty, the sounds in my life pull me back to the vibrant present. Linnea, with her pudgy hand wrapped around my calloused finger, speaks of the marvels beneath our feet, the importance of curiosity and the joy of wonder. Autumn skies stirred by the crane's ancient voice beat a rhythm echoing beyond the span of my own life, beyond even the birth of our species. In my darkest days I often turn to my bookshelf, hungry for the light held within thumb-worn pages.

My copy of Frankl's *Man's Search for Meaning* is tattered, each page cluttered with notes and highlighted sentences. Frankl and his fellow prisoners in a Nazi concentration camp were literally stripped to naked existence. All possessions gone. Wives, mothers, fathers, brothers, sisters, children—gone. The hair on their heads and bodies shaved, names replaced by numbers tattooed on their arms.

Frankl writes of a particularly brutal day deep into his imprisonment; a day beginning with a predawn forced march over frozen ground, the guards driving them on with the butts of their rifles. Frankl occasionally glanced up from the icy puddles to glimpse the sky where the pink light of the dawn was beginning to spread behind a dark bank of clouds. "But my mind," recalls Frankl, "clung to my wife's image, imagining it with uncanny acuteness. I heard her answering me, saw her smile, her frank and encouraging look. Real or not, her look was then more luminous than the sun which was beginning to rise. I understood how a man who has nothing left in this world still may know bliss, be it only for a brief moment, in the contemplation of his beloved." Sliding Frankl's words back onto the shelf, I believe there is no future imaginable that does not leave room for the possibility of generosity and grace.

In the months before Linnea's birth, I quit trying to save the world. I'd become blinded by the drive to do more than I possibly could. In the mad rush to undo the ravages of the industrial revolution, I was foolish enough to gauge the value of my efforts in the shallow rhetoric of political debate and narrow world of senate votes.

I no longer count votes and plot paths to victories. I have little interest in battle plans and deliverables, policies and outcomes. It is the act of speaking itself that matters. My affection for cranes bonds me to places and people wherever those birds fly. My fondness for Lemesurier Island resonates through everyone who has opened their hearts to a specific place. Traveling in defense of the Arctic Refuge connects me with the wide, vibrant community of folks cleaning creeks, restoring forests, and marveling at birds in every river bottom and mountaintop across this continent.

I now believe even the extinction of cranes cannot render efforts at conservation irrelevant anymore than the death of a soldier can strip meaning from calls for peace. From the nuns in Indiana to friends gathered in Senator Kerry's office, from the Dog of God in Cochabamba to my father's tears on a quiet Alaskan hillside, I hear echoes of a long, seamless thread of voices speaking for what they love. Not until I add my voice to the chorus do I know I am not alone. Not until I speak out do I believe that we are, in Annie Dillard's words, "ordinary beads on a never-ending string."

———

Steve was Frank's best friend. It made tragic sense that he was the one to pull Anya's father from the sea. What did not make sense was the doctor's report. It all started with just a headache. A visit to the local clinic turned into a sudden flight to a Seattle oncologist. Anya was still in medical school then, and she joined Steve's wife and two young boys in the waiting room as surgeons removed the tumor. A year later, when the tumor grew back, Anya followed Steve into the operating room for the second surgery. She held his hand as they opened his skull. She kept holding as they projected images on the ceiling and asked Steve questions, probing his brain, searching for the line between lethal tumor and essential tissue.

The operation bought time but not enough. Anya and I helped nurse Steve through his last days. He died at night and we kept his body in the house until the following evening. His young boys crawled into the bed and washed their father's body. All the grace, tenderness, love, and care with which those boys bathed their dad could not bring life back into a body growing colder by the minute. There was no material justification for cleaning Steve up. He was, after all, on the way to the crematorium. Those boys were not looking for promises nor hoping for miracles. They were groping for connection to a father who could no longer pitch a baseball.

"Hope, however feeble its foundation," writes David James Duncan, "bespeaks allegiance to every unlikely beauty that remains on earth." When Miriam lost her mind, her allegiance to beauty was laid bare. Free to focus on anything, her gaze fell to the flash of wings, a swirl of paint, a snippet of song. Frankl escaped the confines of imprisonment through the tunnel of his allegiance to his wife. Mary, tossed into bottomless grief by Jonny's fall, was caught by an allegiance to grieving women around the world. The care guiding those warm sponges over cold flesh provided a direction for the long slow path through grief.

We strengthen our allegiance to beauty by taking care of our bodies even though they will shrivel, in caring for our minds even though we may lose them, in bathing the dead even though they will not come back to life, in pushing leaves into the mouths of dead deer, in teaching our children to love that which may one day vanish.

Miriam had no way of knowing she gave the stranger in her room the gift of her joy. No way of understanding the hope she kindled behind the one door, the escape, from the doughnut of terror. Frankl recalls that, "We who lived in the concentration camps can remember the men who walked through the huts comforting others, giving away their last piece of bread. They may have been few in number but they offer sufficient proof that everything can be taken from a man but one thing: the last of the human freedoms—to choose one's attitude in any given set of circumstances, to choose one's own way."

If every step of one's way is along a path of caring, does it matter what the future brings? Whatever changes come to our little town, whatever befalls our spinning planet, Anya will still be baking pies, soothing the sick, laughing with her daughter, tending her garden, and knitting warm hats and cozy sweaters. Linnea's way, so far, is guided by a mix of curiosity and goofiness, compassion and laughter. She'll brood over the tragedy of war all afternoon but by teeth-brushing time end up spraying toothpaste all over the counter in a fit of giggles. She is, like me, saddened by the new snowmobiles in town, the whine of engines smothering the song of winter wrens. But she is also quick to sing, to make her own music. She'll cry for a deer's death but lift her voice in gratitude, tears still wet on her cheeks.

If lamenting the loss of beauty is itself a beautiful act, can beauty really ever diminish?

"The only spiritually responsible way I know to be a citizen, artist, or activist," writes Duncan, "is by giving little or no thought to things such as saving the planet, achieving world peace, or stopping neocon greed. Great things seem to be undoable things. Small things, lovingly done, are always within our reach."

I want to find a way to reflect the gifts of my family and friends. I want to breathe life into the wisdom bound within the dog-eared pages on my bookshelf. I want to grow carrots not because agribusiness is a filthy, greedy, heartless beast but because rooting in the dirt is fun, worms are groovy creatures, and you can't buy the sweet satisfaction of a fresh carrot at any price. I want to live a simple, rooted life not because my place of privilege is responsible for poverty but because meals of venison, potatoes, and nagoonberry pie fill our kitchen with gratitude-crazed grins. I want to leave the Subaru in the driveway not because the carbon spilling from the exhaust will tip the planet into an inferno but because a bike ride puts wind in our faces and birdsong in our ears; it pumps blood through our veins and reminds us all that life is a dizzyingly splendid idea.

Two weeks ago I poked a row of holes beneath our pea fence. The soil was still cool, the worms moving slow after the long winter. Linnea carefully dropped a green pea into each finger-size opening and then pinched it closed.

Yesterday I decided the dirt was warm enough to plant the rest of the garden. Fresh back from a day of kindergarten, Linnea joined me between the freshly turned rows. A recently arrived yellow-rumped warbler chattered from the willow tree. A ruby-crowned kinglet called from the forest edge. The chunky, rough seeds of beets were easy to grasp between finger and thumb and plant one at a time. The smaller spinach seeds took more patience to get properly spaced. I'd just filled the bowl of Linnea's palm with the tiny oblong kernels of carrot seeds when the cranes called. My daughter wrapped the seeds in her little fist and stood straight to search the sky. Fifty or so birds in a high wavering line sliced the pale spring sky.

After they passed, we turned back to the carrot row. "These seeds are so small you have to just sprinkle them—let them fall where they may," I said.

"Like this, Papa?"

"Yep. Just like that."

An afternoon westerly swept through the tumbling seeds. We'll likely end up with feathery sprouts in the next row over, mixed in with the broad leaves of radishes and kale.

Small acts done with great love are like tiny seeds in a gusty breeze; you can't know where they will take hold or what they will grow. Sow enough of them and they will show up in the most unlikely places. If they grow thick, you may be lucky enough to be left singing when all else is stripped away.

THANKS

———

AT FIRST LIGHT each hunter throws back the last gulp of coffee, shrugs into a day pack, and trudges into the woods. We spend the day alone—testing the wind, looking for tracks, hoping for a glimpse of fur. The setting sun drives us one by one back to the light and warmth of the cabin. As each hunter kicks off their boots and hangs damp clothes around the stove, they share the day's observations. The long evenings fill, as they always do, with an endless roll of questions.

What elevation did you guys see the most sign? Wasn't that a squirrely wind in the back of the valley? When a deer catches your scent and runs off, how far do you think it goes? Anybody else see twin fawns? How many winter kill carcasses did you see?

Pooling individual insights is like being in multiple places at once and seeing things you could never notice on your own. The communal observations enhance individual success; with all those eyes in the woods we're often able to figure out where the deer are congregated. We also pool the gift of meat. A bit of one person's good luck ends up in everyone's freezer.

My friend Richard, a keen naturalist and compulsive note taker, has recorded the details of our decades-long inquiry into the habits and habitat of deer in his field journal. This book is a journal of sorts, a chronicle of an ongoing inquiry about how to keep the diminishment of beauty from making us less alive. I am blessed to be steeped in a rich and far-flung dialogue. It happens around campfires and in the post office, on the roadside and in the woods, through letters and books. I am grateful for the insights I'd never have reached on my own. The conversation is expanding and involves too many people to thank them all—below are but a few.

Thanks to Richard Carstensen for being a scribe, for keeping so much from being lost to the winds of memory. I am grateful for your forest companionship and the meat lumps cooked in the woods after my wedding ceremony.

Thanks to Kim Heacox for the cold beers and hot music nights, for believing we are funnier than we might actually be, and for listening together to KFCK radio.

Thanks to Bob Christensen for teaching me that hoarding protects nothing and paradise is too precious not to share.

Thanks to Mary Cook for showing me there can be power in surrender, beauty found at the bottom of grief.

Thanks to Scott Russell Sanders and Kathleen Dean Moore for friendship, wisdom, encouraging words, and willingness to read my manuscript not once, but twice.

Thanks to Libby Roderick for her clear voice and that convertible ride in the rain, coats zipped tight, heater and the 24-hour Elvis station turned up high. Thanks to Richard Nelson for having no patience for worry, for dedicating every breath to the celebration of the world's beauties. Thanks to Carolyn Servid who, when I called with a hair-brained idea, could have said no but didn't. Thanks to Judy Maier for encouraging me to travel and welcoming my return. Thanks to Nat Drumheller for all the hours and miles devoted to studying the birds of Gustavus. Thanks to Greg Streveler for the loan of a shovel and plot of fertile ground; I am still harvesting things from that garden planted so many years ago.

Thanks for the folks who have joined me around the pile of bones: Steve Merli, Jai Crapella, Jake Jacoby, Miller White, Sean Neilson, Kathy Lochman, as well as many of the folks already mentioned above.

Thanks to Kate Rogers for believing in this story and checking in on my progress. Thanks to all who read bits and pieces of the text and provided helpful feedback: Dawn Marano, Joan Gregory, Michelene Marcom, Chris Gabrielle, Paul Berry, Phoebe Vanselow, Emily Mount, Melanie Heacox, Jen Marlow, and Molly May. Thanks to all the people and groups dedicated to keeping public lands public. Without your efforts the trees of Lemesurier Island and Frank's Mountain would have been run through the mill of private profit long ago. Special thanks to Cindy Shogun at the Alaska Wilderness League for dusting me off and ushering me through the halls of Congress. Thanks to Mike Eaton for being a gracious host and all his work to ensure cranes have enough corn to get through the winter.

Thanks to Mary Lentfer, my mother, for all the hand-written cards expressing pride with every oddball, unconventional choice I have made; I have saved them all. (Never underestimate the power of a mother's pride.) Thanks to Jack Lentfer, my father, for all the times he got us lost in the woods and found the way home again.

Thanks to Linnea Rain for having a weirdo-pants papa and not wanting it any other way. And deep thanks to Anya Maier, the steady force behind all the best decisions in my life.

HANK LENTFER, A LIFE-LONG ALASKAN, is a gardener, hunter, woodworker, and musician. He helped establish and now manages the Gustavus Forelands Preserve, a four-thousand acre refuge for migratory sandhill cranes. His writing has appeared in *Orion*, *Wilderness*, and several anthologies including *Moral Ground: Ethical Action for a Planet in Peril*. He is co-editor of *Arctic Refuge: A Circle of Testimony*. When not in the woodshop, garden, or at his desk, he's hiking through the rainforest or lying in a meadow watching cranes. His website is www.hanklentfer.com.

Other Titles You Might Enjoy by The Mountaineers Books

A Long Trek Home:
4,000 Miles by Boot, Raft, and Ski
Erin McKittrick
A harrowing account of this unprecedented trek
from Seattle to the Aleutian Islands

Steller's Island: Adventures
of a Pioneer Naturalist in Alaska
Dean Littlepage
A fascinating story of 18th-century naturalist, Georg
Steller, and his discoveries along the north coast of
North America

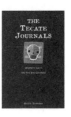

The Tecate Journals:
Seventy Days on the Rio Grande
Keith Bowden
A compelling and timely exploration of an
important natural resource and its impact
on our borderlands

Pickets and Dead Men: Seasons on Rainier
Bree Loewen
A funny and hair-raising story of a young
woman's experience as a climbing ranger

Kissing Kilimanjaro:
Leaving It All on Top of Africa
Daniel Dorr
Find out how far one man will go to impress a woman
and conquer Africa's highest mountain.

The Mountaineers Books has more than
500 outdoor recreation titles in print.
For details, visit
www.mountaineersbooks.org.